The Music Business
Contract Library

HAL•LEONARD®

Hal Leonard Books
An Imprint of Hal Leonard Corporation
New York

Published in 2008 by Hal Leonard Books
An Imprint of Hal Leonard Corporation
7777 West Bluemound Road
Milwaukee, WI 53213

Trade Book Division Editorial Offices
19 West 21st Street, New York, NY 10010

Printed in USA

Book design by Stephen Ramirez

Library of Congress Cataloging-in-Publication Data is available upon request.

ISBN 978-1-4234-5458-8

www.halleonard.com

To Cindy Terry, Bobby Rector, Terry and Sarah Penney,
Tom Morrell, Walter Hyatt, Jesse Taylor,
Jamie Lee Bradford, Gene Bullard, and Tim Garon

CONTENTS

Part I: Getting Started

Part II: Teaming Up

Part III: The Professionals

Part IV: The Future

PREFACE

My old saying that every artist who got screwed in the music industry got screwed in writing appears to be holding up in the early twenty-first century. Although the Internet and consumer electronics are changing the emerging artist's paradigm for promotion, delivery and playback, the product—a song performance—remains the same. The legal foundations for the creation, ownership, and exploitation of music as an art form remain for the most part unchanged. Internet or not, a copyright is still a copyright and a publishing, recording or management deal can still make or break your career if you don't know what you're doing.

The artists that I have found to be the most successful in their careers were the ones that:

► Treated their music as a business.

► Worked a bit harder and longer at the business.

► Never stopped growing and evolving as artists.

It may be a cruel way to view the music industry but that song, that performance, that work of art is a commodity. Yes, it is your baby—it is beautiful and you are the proud parent but will it win a beauty contest? If you are a performing artist, you are the product being marketed. If you are a songwriter, the song is the commodity. If you are an engineer, producer, attorney, publicist, agent, or other support professional, it is your talent, network, experience, and knowledge you are selling. It is important to decide what the product is in a given situation. As an example, it would be a waste of time to promote your performance skills to a publisher during a song pitch. An old adage in Nashville when hearing a 60-second guitar intro in a song pitch is, "Don't bore us. Where's the chorus?" This is not to say that clueless entertainment business rubes don't get lucky sometimes and get to the top—they just make a lot less money than their better-educated and represented counterparts.

You don't have to be an intellectual to create an intellectual property—just a good writer or performer. How many of Einstein's hit tunes come to mind? The intellectual property you create in your song or performance becomes the product that is bought and sold. It has a name and a price or at least a perceived value. The difference between your perceived value and the person on the other side of the table's perception is the front line. Negotiating the terms of the sale is your job. Information is also a precious commodity and the more of it you have working for you, the better your negotiating position. A casual attitude toward your entertainment career will generally yield casual results.

I am not an attorney but since I began publishing and commenting on the deals that have crossed my desk and those of friends, I have garnered some knowledge in what can make a deal work and what can break the deal. This book is meant to be a map through the jungle of this business but, as all true adventurers know, when you get into uncharted territory, it is best to hire a native guide. That native guide is an entertainment attorney.

You might be saying to yourself, "Hey dude, I bought this book so I wouldn't have to spend money on an attorney!" It is my hope that you will save lots of legal fees and problems using this book—you can perform many of the legal tasks in your career using nothing but this book. A good rule of thumb is to call an attorney the second you hit a clause in a contract that seems unclear, unfair, or unintelligible. Major deals are quite detailed; new methods of delivery and licensing are evolving almost daily. Does your last record or distribution deal include HDTV and BlueRay clauses? Are you to be paid the same royalty for every kind of product and delivery in every region? The business is changing faster now than at any time in the past and one of the primary jobs of an entertainment attorney or savvy management is to stay on top of all the legal ramifications that come with each new technology.

Using this book you will be able to have a first meeting with an attorney that will be productive and cost-effective. You've done your homework and know the basics and essential parts of the deal. You will not be paying someone $200 an hour to explain, usually in a slow cadence and at great (billable) detail, how to copyright a song.

When negotiating with others, you want to build a productive and prosperous relationship with both parties striving to come to agreement on what they can both view as fair. Everyone negotiates in good faith and with impeccable ethics. Not. This touchy-feely approach has sunk many a career ship. Whether you are looking for a label, a manager, or any other significant professional partner, keep in mind that the job of your legal opponent is to get what you've got at the lowest possible price. Cool office, nice guy or not, you should approach these new relationships much like you would a blind date—with a good dose of skepticism. At the offset and until proven otherwise, view the relationship as adversarial—the person you are negotiating with is not in the business of looking out for your best interests; you are.

In this book and CD-ROM I will try to address the most common aspects of an evolving career. I will have a few cohorts and friends clock in with advice and anecdotes; sharing what worked or didn't work under different circumstances. Each aspect of the industry—the artist, the song, the recording—all have similarities at the base of the deal but there are different properties and rights being conveyed in each module. The deals are similar and yet not the same. We will address the similarities first, and then break down the specifics of each type of deal as the artist's career progresses. "Know thy enemy" is not only good military strategy it is good business strategy—if you can put yourself successfully into the mind and viewpoint of your negotiating opponent, you will gain insight to possible common ground, carrots you can dangle to help the deal proceed, or pitfalls and traps being laid for you. More so than in any arena, knowledge is power at the negotiating table.

Disclaimer: This book and its accompanying CD-ROM is designed to give the reader an overview of the legalities of the entertainment and music industry and is not to be construed as legal advice in regard to any legal or business situation. The information in this book is meant as a general guideline only. Entertainment and music law changes at a very rapid rate and the contents of this book will not reflect changes in the industry since its publication.

The reader is strongly advised to seek experienced and competent legal counsel before entering into any agreement that could have long-term effects on your career or your intellectual properties.

ACKNOWLEDGMENTS

I would like to acknowledge the following people for their help and support

For bringing me to the table:
Mike Lawson at Hal Leonard

For making me appear literate:
Yvonne Perry at Writers in the Sky

The Thick or Thin Gang

Joe Mann and Suzanne Freeman, Ronnie and Amy Leatherman, Deborah Dennis, Nancy Rector, Linda Bullard, Gary Wimmer, Karyn Lyn, Alex Abravanel, Ron and Linda Fujiu, Mojo Mickey Lees & Erika, Rand and Barbara McCullough, Stan Morris and the Melody Corner, Blake Olsen, Jay Boy Adams, The Don Strange Family, Gabriel McCormick and David Lawhorn and the whole Welfare Café Gang, Ron Knuth, Larry and Cindy Wilkerson, James Harvey, Alamo Springs Café, Claude "Butch" Morgan, Bill Davis and Dash Rip Rock, Will Owen-Gage, Susan Owen, Monica Smith, Natalie Steele, Jennifer King, Kathleen Hudson and Gordon Ames

WHAT'S ON THE CD-ROM

The CD-ROM accompanying this book has a large library of contracts, forms, and spreadsheets to help you in your quest for music industry success. The contracts are in four formats: Microsoft Word DOC (versions 2000 XP), Adobe Acrobat™ PDF, Rich Text Files RTF for importing into other word processors that may not be compatible with Word, and simple ASCII text (TXT) files. Note: For the PDF files you must have Adobe Reader installed on your computer.

There may be some differences in how the contracts display on your computer depending on your operating system, word processing software, your video display, and printer settings. The easiest way to get started using the library is to just browse your way through it. Getting started is a breeze—just click on the file "index.html" at the root of the CD-ROM. This will fire up your browser to give you to the Quick Start menu.

From there, you can click on each of the four buttons to navigate your way through each section of the library. Each section has the content listed in the various formats and you will be one click away from viewing the documents.

THE CONTRACTS

When you click on the contracts button, you will see a listing of each contract in the library with the various file types you can access. Just click on the contract and format type you want.

Just scroll down the page until you find the document you're looking for and click on the appropriate button. Let's take a look at the forms part of the library.

THE FORMS

The forms are in PDF format only and are documents from the Library of Congress and fill-in-the-blank forms for such things as band inventories, partner sharing percentages, and such. This is where you will find the Library of Congress copyright forms for a variety of intellectual properties including song, recording, video, and graphic arts forms. Some of the forms are worksheets for band inventories, net worth, and profit/loss projections. If the form is something that can be calculated, there will also be a copy in the next section, "The Spreadsheets."

THE SPREADSHEETS

These spreadsheets are in two formats: XLS for users of Microsoft Excel and compatible products and PDF for Adobe Acrobat users. Unlike the forms library, all the formulas are intact in the spreadsheets and they are fully modifiable if you want to expand the spreadsheets with your own information and formulas.

WEB RESOURCES

Using the Web menu you will be able to link to the major player's Web sites including all the writer and performance arts associations and guilds. These links can come in handy. If you need a song clearance you can just click on Harry Fox or songfile.com, credit card in hand and have a song clearance document in minutes instead of weeks. You can also check these sites for changes in law such as the statutory mechanical rate for using a song you didn't write that Congress increases every few years.

CD-ROM DIRECTORY CONTENTS

If you would like to explore the CD-ROM outside the browser interface, the directory structure is as follows:

Forms Directory

This directory contains all the forms broken down in to subfolders ASCAP_APP which contains ASCAP writer and publisher applications, BMI_CLR which contains the BMI forms, IRS and LOC which contains the Library of Congress forms.

Open Office

This directory contains installations for both Mac and PC for the open source office solution from Sun Microsystems, Inc.. Open Office contains programs similar to what is found in Microsoft Office and other similar products. The Word and Excel files can all be opened and manipulated using this software suite.

PDF

This directory contains all the contracts and forms in PDF format. You will need Adobe Reader to open the documents. You can download Adobe Reader free on the Web by visiting http://www.adobe.com.

RTF

This is where you will find the contract library in rich text format which will make the library compatible with other word processors. If you are using a non-mainstream word processor, this might be the route for you as the document formatting (bold, underline, etc.) remains intact.

Sheets

This directory contains all the spreadsheets in Excel 2000 XP format. These sheets contain active formulas and macros to make your calculating as easy as possible. There are two sub-directories: XLS for the spreadsheets and PDF for the Acrobat files.

TXT

This directory contains all the contract files and some of the forms in straight ASCII text files. All document formatting such as bold, italics and coloration have all been stripped from these files making them easy to cut and paste into any application without any formatting conflicts.

Web

This directory contains the pages and images that comprise the CD-ROM's mini Web site. In the addendums directory you will find three Web-based tutorials on the basics of management, publishing, and finance.

Word

This directory contains all the contract documents and text-based forms in Microsoft Word™ format. These files are backwardly compatible with versions of Word back to Office 2000.

DOCUMENTS BY CATEGORY

Another way to view the library is to look at it by categories. Some of the contracts can be used in multiple categories but here is a listing of just a few examples of the basic necessities by category.

Songwriter

Musician Personal Inventory
Publisher—Exclusive Writer Agreement
Publisher—Single Song 1
Publisher—Single Song Option
FORM PA—Copyright a Song
FORM SR—Copyright a Recording

Performing Artist or Band

Booking—Casual Band Agreement
Booking—Artist Technical Rider
Booking—Special Event/Concert 1
Consignment Agreement 1
Exclusive Agent/Artist Agreement
Publicist Agreement

Recording Artist or Band

Receipt for Master Recording
Recording—Management/Indie 360
Recording—Budget Worksheet
Video Release (recorded performance)

ALPHABETICAL LISTING OF FILES AND FORMATS

Name of File	Type	Format Included
Actor Share of Net	contract	Word, PDF, txt
Assignment of Copyright 1	contract	Word, PDF, txt
Assignment of Copyright 2	contract	Word, PDF, txt
Assignment of Copyright 3	contract	Word, PDF, txt
Assignment of Copyright 4	contract	Word, PDF, txt
Band Inventory Form	worksheet	Excel, PDF
Band Inventory Worksheet 1	worksheet	Excel, PDF
Band Monthly Income Expense	worksheet	Excel, PDF
Booking—AGVA Booking Agreement	contract	Word, PDF, txt
Booking—Artist Technical Rider	contract	Word, PDF, txt
Booking—Casual Band Agreement	contract	Word, PDF, txt
Booking—Special Event/Concert 1	contract	Word, PDF, txt
Booking—Special Event/Concert 2	contract	Word, PDF, txt
Booking—Special Event/Concert 3	contract	Word, PDF, txt
Booking—Venue Agreement	contract	Word, PDF, txt
Certificate of Limited Partnership	contract	Word, PDF, txt
Commercial (Jingle) Agreement 1	contract	Word, PDF, txt
Commercial (Jingle) Agreement 2	contract	Word, PDF, txt
Consignment Agreement 1	contract	Word, PDF, txt
Co-Promotion Agreement	contract	Word, PDF, txt
Daily Expense Report	worksheet	Excel, PDF
Distribution 1	contract	Word, PDF, txt
Distribution 2	contract	Word, PDF, txt
Duplicator Indemnity	contract	Word, PDF, txt
Duplicator Indemnity (Short Form)	contract	Word, PDF, txt
Exclusive Agent/Artist Agreement	contract	Word, PDF, txt
Executive Employment	contract	Word, PDF, txt
Feature Film Offering	contract	Word, PDF, txt
Film Call Sheet	contract	Word, PDF, txt
Film Synchronization 1	contract	Word, PDF, txt
Film/Video Release 1	contract	Word, PDF, txt
Foreign Agent 1	contract	Word, PDF, txt
General Partnership Agreement	contract	Word, PDF, txt

Name of File	Type	Format Included
General Radio Broadcast Release 1	contract	Word, PDF, txt
License from Publisher for General Use	contract	Word, PDF, txt
Limited Partnership 1	contract	Word, PDF, txt
Literary Option Agreement	contract	Word, PDF, txt
Management 1	contract	Word, PDF, txt
Management 2 Spec/360	contract	Word, PDF, txt
Manager Monthly Worksheet	worksheet	Excel, PDF
Musician Personal Inventory	worksheet	Excel, PDF
Non-Disclosure 1	contract	Word, PDF, txt
Non-Disclosure 2	contract	Word, PDF, txt
Non-Disclosure 3	contract	Word, PDF, txt
Non-Disclosure 4	contract	Word, PDF, txt
Photo Work for Hire 1	contract	Word, PDF, txt
Photo Work for Hire 2	contract	Word, PDF, txt
Producer 1—General Production Agreement	contract	Word, PDF, txt
Producer 2—General Production Agreement	contract	Word, PDF, txt
Producer 3—Short Form Speculative	contract	Word, PDF, txt
Producer 4—Short Form Simple	contract	Word, PDF, txt
Producer 5—Production/Promotion Agreement	contract	Word, PDF, txt
Producer—Lien on Master	contract	Word, PDF, txt
Producer—Spec Royalty Rider	contract	Word, PDF, txt
Production—Lien on Project	contract	Word, PDF, txt
Production—Promissory Note	contract	Word, PDF, txt
Production—Promotion Agreement	contract	Word, PDF, txt
Property Release for Film/Video	contract	Word, PDF, txt
Publicist Agreement	contract	Word, PDF, txt
Publisher—Sub-publishing 1	contract	Word, PDF, txt
Publisher—Sub-publishing Foreign	contract	Word, PDF, txt
Publisher—Exclusive Writer Agreement	contract	Word, PDF, txt
Publisher—Mechanical 1	contract	Word, PDF, txt
Publisher—Mechanical 2	contract	Word, PDF, txt
Publisher—Royalty Payment Schedule	contract	Word, PDF, txt
Publisher—Royalty Sharing	contract	Word, PDF, txt
Publisher—Single Song 1	contract	Word, PDF, txt
Publisher—Single Song 2	contract	Word, PDF, txt
Publisher—Single Song Option	contract	Word, PDF, txt

Name of File	Type	Format Included
Radio Program Live Broadcast Release	contract	Word, PDF, txt
Radio Program Prerecorded Broadcast Release	contract	Word, PDF, txt
Receipt for Master Recording	contract	Word, PDF, txt
Recording—Management/Indie 360	contract	Word, PDF, txt
Recording—Budget Worksheet	worksheet	Excel, PDF
Recording—Indie Compilation	contract	Word, PDF, txt
Recording—Indie Short Form	contract	Word, PDF, txt
Sound Contracting	contract	Word, PDF, txt
Sponsorship 1	contract	Word, PDF, txt
Sponsorship 2	contract	Word, PDF, txt
Standard Location Release (Film/Video)	contract	Word, PDF, txt
Track License (Film/Video) 1	contract	Word, PDF, txt
Track License (Film/Video) 2	contract	Word, PDF, txt
Video Release (Minor Option)	contract	Word, PDF, txt
Video Release (Recorded Performance)	contract	Word, PDF, txt
Video/Film Property Release	contract	Word, PDF, txt
Vocalist Agreement	contract	Word, PDF, txt
Yearly Profit/Loss Worksheet	worksheet	Excel, PDF

INTRODUCTION

The entertainment industry is changing almost every day. With the constant deployment of new technologies, the legal status of art as a commodity is being constantly redefined both at the negotiating table and in the courts. The paradigms and "boiler plate" deals of the past are fast fading into irrelevance, but many of the underlying principles regarding the ownership and exploitation of intellectual property are still as valid as ever. The song, the artist, and everything that goes along with an entertainment package are still the commodities to be exploited, marketed, and hopefully profited upon.

We will be looking at the foundations of a number of deals both good and bad. In my previous offerings, I have focused on career self-defense techniques for artists and musicians. I paid no mind to the ancillary industries such as management, publishing, engineering, and other jobs that make the music industry work. This time out, I will be looking at the points of negotiation from both sides of the table each step of the way in hopes that those who can't carry a tune in a bucket can still carry the heavy weight for their artist clients. For every talent on a national stage there are dozens of support personnel with career needs that also need to be addressed.

The contract examples we will be using are from my filing cabinet and cover more than three decades of wheeling and dealing in the music industry. What has changed to a great degree is the complexity of the agreements that artists are entering into.

This is primarily being driven by new technologies such as CDs, DVDs, HD, the Internet, and other digital delivery systems. At times, it almost crosses the line into science fiction when you see newly developed contracts.

Twenty years ago you would license a property to "the entire world." Ten years ago it was "the entire universe." I have seen contracts recently that stipulate, "The entire universe or any universes that now exist or may come into being." That is really covering your bases; perhaps to optimistic excess. CD sales in the ninth dimension have been slow to date but hope springs eternal.

Although trying to cover as many bases as I can, we will be focusing much of this dialog on the emergence of what I see as the most positive development in the industry ever: the independent artist who is *not* looking for a major label deal. In the past, the only way to success was getting picked up by a major or large independent label. When the Internet leveled the playing field for music promotion, a new player emerged in the industry—the artist that can make a good living without the financial help or artistic guidance of corporate accounts and A&R personnel. When looking at the prospect of fame and fortune, many emerging contemporary artists have chosen fortune above fame. It turns out that you can be just a little famous and make good money—or at least more than many of your major label counterparts. New independent artists and their teams have generated sales that are the envy of a major label new artist. Why? My theory of why it works is multifaceted.

► The artists are closer to their fan base and can actually utilize fans for promotions. In many cases, the fan becomes an active participant in the artist's success.

► The artist can try new and innovative marketing techniques outside the box of traditional promotions that aren't taught to Harvard MBAs.

► There is higher value returned to the music consumer without the layers of corporate control that have nothing to do with music but are guided by the principals of bottom line quarterly corporate accounting. Fans feel they are supporting art rather than a large multinational.

▶ The elimination of the middle-men in a direct artist-to-consumer paradigm leaves more money in the pocket of the artist or indie label for further investment in the commodity and planning for the future is much easier and more reliable.

I am not an attorney. As I mentioned previously, the legal landscape of our industry is a constantly moving target. Innovative deals emerge every day and it is impossible to keep up with every technological advance when writing a book. I had to laugh when reviewing contracts from the '70s that had terms like, "upon cylinder, phonograph, or talking machine records." That was emerging technology at some point in time, but it would look pretty silly in today's legal landscape. That is why music and entertainment attorneys will always be around and can be your strongest ally in career advancement if they know what they are doing. They can also be your worst enemy if they don't. It is always a good starting point when negotiating to assume that the other guy's attorney knows what he is doing; regardless of you or your attorney's bona fides.

IT ALL STARTS WITH YOU

This phrase has been the moniker for all the books I've written because in my experience, that is what entertainment industry success boils down to: your talent, your conviction, your persistence, and your very hard work. This applies not only to performing artists, songwriters, and other creative people but to the technical, promotional, accounting, legal, and other support personnel that drive both the show and the wheels of commerce. You will have to give your all when competing against like-minded artists who are taking no prisoners. Camaraderie and collaboration are great and desirable, but remember many if not most of those competing in this business want blood and red meat—your blood. Let's see if we can avoid spilling too much on our road to success.

Part I

Getting Started

CHAPTER 1

Defining Your Goals, Product, and Image

Will Owen Gage, Courtesy of The Music Office

Every year thousands of new independent artists release new music to the world and the major label releases number in the hundreds. Needless to say there is a lot of competition out there for fans, listeners, and media outlets. You are going to have to mix it up with your competitors—not necessarily in a ruthless manner—but you will have to keep moving fast and be creative at the very least.

Musicians are a lot like people in the film industry; they always have a "deal" in the works. "We opened a dialog with a major label this week" could easily mean they called and got the mailing address to send the demo. "We're working on the new CD" could mean they bought the first microphone for the project studio.

As a consultant and producer, when it comes to what I think about many new acts, I keep my opinion to myself. It is generally not complimentary in nature. Shortly into our first meeting I can see that this band is clueless. In the band's mind though, they see the future clear as the azure skies of a summer afternoon. They are in a stadium before swarms of screaming fans thanking Sting for opening for them. What I see is a band breakup within months as the lead singer's girlfriend is winking at the bass player when the band's attention is elsewhere. You don't have to be very savvy to discern the bullet from the bull.

Speaking of bull, you will have to learn to wade in it if you want be a player in this business and become a master of shameless self-promotion. You never tell anyone outside the band that things are going nowhere fast and the band is withering on the vine. It is a fact of life that you have to keep your business associates and the public in promotional hip waders throughout your career.

How will you define yourself as an artist or a representative or contractor for an artist? The following few paragraphs may sound like old adages, but regardless of what role you will be playing in this drama of the music industry, there are a few things that will be required for success at any level.

Talent, Capability, and Competence. Talent is what drives this business. Musical talent, engineering, promotional, and management talent all come to play. The performers aren't the only stars in this business. After Millie Vanilli's lip-sync Grammy a few decades back, we all have to admit that talent isn't always a necessary part of a popular entertainment package. In Vanilli's case, talent wasn't necessary but he still had to look good on camera and lip-sync convincingly. A sound or recording engineer's personal appearance or musical capabilities are unimportant but they need to know how to tweak a knob and bring out the best in an artist's performance.

Whatever claim you stake on the music industry terrain, try to be the best in your genre or field—at least at a local or regional level. Learn from others and stay on top of what's happening. Never forget you are competing and the other players are serious and are playing for keeps.

Reliability. Concert venues like bands that show up on time and ready to rock. Record labels like master recordings delivered when the contract specifies. Band members appreciate not waiting for a member late to rehearsal. Bands like club owners that pay what was agreed upon and agents like their commissions in a timely manner. I could go on and on but you get my drift. Many times, I have seen the career of an incredibly talented individual torpedoed by the same talent's unreliability. If a performer is late to a recording session, the clock is rolling, money and time are wasting, and people who could be creating are twiddling their thumbs waiting for someone who deems their own convenience more important than others' time. I view time as not only money but as a non-renewable resource that each of us is allotted a certain amount of. Wasting my time is stealing part of my future.

Honesty and Integrity. Many would fault me for including these two words in the same paragraph with the music industry or politics, but the fact of the matter is that your long-term success is built on everyone winning to some degree and building business and legal relationships that last. The industry is full of dishonest people trying to exploit you and some are wildly successful. Over time, however, you will be drawn to repeat business with those who have treated you fairly and equitably. People will be inclined to conduct repeat business with you or forge artistic relationships if you are trustworthy. Even though there are thousands of players in the business, the business is like a small town and your bad reputation can travel much farther than you might think. When two other people are talking about you, how do you want to come off to them?

Some parts of this industry are time-sensitive and deadline-oriented. Film and television scores have to be delivered on time. Any delay can cost an incredible amount of money. If you are collaborating on a deadline project, you want to make sure your partner is reliable and will deliver the goods on time.

Flexibility. The road to music success is littered with potholes and speed bumps. Well-laid plans sometimes have to be modified or even discarded on the run. Sometimes you have no room to be flexible, but if you can make an accommodation for a business associate, do it. It can only generate good will.

DEFINING GOALS

Having a game plan is essential to building any career. You don't have to start with the whole career-spanning game plan in place; just a plan that will get you to the finish line of your next goal in the big picture. Break the long term into components. The first thing that a musician or writer should work on is their chops. If you are going to be a performing professional you will need to be competitive with other artists and bands at the same level you are on. Hone your skills.

Let's start with the assumption that you are a performer ready to leave the garage. There is more than one path to success, depending on which fork in the road you will be traveling. A pop performer or songwriter would have a different career strategy than a classical performer or composer. There are legalities for both careers and many similarities but the audience, marketing, and goals may be vastly different.

The First Ensemble aka The Garage Band

The vast majority of musicians will be performing and building their careers playing in bands. There are exceptions. Some singer-songwriters, most notably on the folk circuit, start their careers as solo artists and essentially remain that way for their entire careers with a few collaborations along the way, but the lion's share of new talent comes out of garages in the form of bands.

It is also very uncommon for a performer to remain with the first band they start out with. The breakup of your first band is almost inevitable as the music progresses and it is revealed that some players have more talent, dedication, or energy than other members. It is not uncommon for a band to fire its most talented member for being a "prima donna." Early on, you will be experimenting with other players to gain knowledge and start building your network. Keep any business arrangements simple, flexible, and revocable.

The first step out of the garage or rehearsal hall is the first gig. As things progress and the band increases its following and performance acumen, legalities should start appearing.

Most casual weekend bands are, whether formally declared such or not, a general partnership. The band members all share equally in the fees received for gigs. There may be small adjustments—gas money, the PA owner getting a bit more but in essence the band, its name, and its revenue are all shared equally. Where does it become a good idea for a band to start to formalize itself in a legal sense? Here are some road signs that might point to contracts in the near future:

▶ The band's earnings reach a point where it is likely or inevitable that the band or its members will start receiving IRS Form 1099 from an agent, venue, or other outside third party or, more often, the band member that the checks are made out to. Cash "under the table" will only go so far in this business—although the life blood of bottom feeders, eventually you will start dealing with other professionals—professionals that want tax write offs and good paper trails of where their money goes. Here's an example:

The Today Tones, a cover band, have a one-year contract with a hotel chain to play the lounge five nights a week for a year. Regardless of whether the contract came from the hotel or its agent, someone will have to sign for the band. This will also be the person who receives the weekly check from the hotel. Imagine the hotel pays the band $2,000 a week. That makes the weekly payroll from the leader of the four-piece band to the three other band members $1,500 a week if all share equally. By year's end, the band leader has received over $100,000 and *shelled out more than $75,000 to the other members. Unless he is very wealthy he will pass on to the IRS that he has paid this in the form of 1099s.*

At this point there is a "leader," a paper trail of booking agreements and a financial trail for the band's activities. If the band is sticking it out long term, this might be the time for a band meeting regarding formalizing the relationship.

A business formation band meeting is in order and might produce something like this:

▶ The band members are all equal members in the band, its name, and business. All decisions will be made by the band. If a majority of the band can't agree on an issue, the issue is taken off the table.

   Example: If three of the four members of a gig don't want to do a specific gig, the band doesn't take it.

▶ The band members all own their own equipment; each member is responsible for their gear.

▶ Band members who bring more than just their instruments into play—PA systems, vans, trucks, and project recording studios come to mind—get compensated at an amount agreed to by the other band members. Example: Jim owns the PA system and van and has to get to the gig before and stay long after the other band members to setup. Jim gets an extra $50 each gig and gas money for any trips out of the area.

▶ A band member can leave at any time, take their toys and go home. The exiting member has no future interest in the band.

▶ All band members share equally in the net revenue. After gas, PA, agent, or other fees, the band members split the money equally.

▶ Any expenses over a certain amount, say $250, has to be approved by a majority of the band.

A more comprehensive and slightly more complex arrangement can be found in the band percentage sharing worksheet in Chapter Four.

Let's look at another scenario—the ensemble that is pulled together by the front person who is choosing the repertoire, booking the gigs and taking care of everything else. The front man is the boss and the members of the band are there at his or her pleasure. There are legalities from both sides of the band under this scenario too. A venue would be a buyer, the band leader or agent would be the contractor, and the band members would be sub-contractors. A front person, the one with the gigs, might have a simple agreement with band members that would address the following issues:

▶ The band, its name, network, and all other assets are the property of the band leader. All decisions, artistic and business, are made by the band leader.

▶ The band member is an independent contractor working at the pleasure of the band leader. The relationship is and shall be, "at will."

▶ All recordings, video, film, and still photography are owned by the band leader. All of the band members' work and contributions to the leader are on a work-for-hire basis and the member will receive no further compensation.

▶ The band member will give the leader their legal name, social security number, and permanent address for tax and accounting purposes.

▶ The band member owns and is responsible for his or her equipment.

▶ The band member can be terminated at any time for any or no reason.

Again, this is a document that could cover less than one page and could double as the new band member's fact sheet. In some cases an artist will build a career with a hot and loyal band as a major component of the product and will make concessions to the band members to keep their loyalty and enthusiasm. An example is where the band leader may get all the record, sponsorship, and writing royalties but will put the band members on a generous year-round salary, pay them a larger cut when performing live, or a combination of both. We will be taking a look at situations like that as we get further down the career path.

WHAT IS THE PRODUCT?

Focus on what you are selling. It could be your talents as a bass player, your skill as a mixer, your songs and voice, or a combination of some or all of these aspects. A singer-songwriter's mission statement might be something like, "I want to put my songs, vision, and voice in front of as many people as possible while making a decent living." Whatever your skill or talent, look at it as the product. It can be distasteful to some artists to have to package themselves into a product that is attractive and compelling to the public. Some musicians think their talent will carry all the weight. All the talent in the world won't help you if nobody knows you exist and the only way to get that visibility is marketing. From your "band members needed" announcement on the bulletin board of the local music store to selling your act to a band leader or club, your job only gets easier when the product and price are clearly defined. Every musician, engineer, producer, or other music pro are all small businesses. There are questions that every small business has to ask itself:

▶ Who else is selling similar products?

▶ How much are they getting for the product?

▶ Who is buying the product and how would I get to them?

These questions are as important to a guitar player starting out as any other new business. If you don't have the chops of the other players in the area and charge $100 a night more, you will probably be spending most of your nights at home. Like it or not, you and your music are now products and must be competitive with other similar products to get anywhere. It is not enough that you believe in the product—you already bought it—you have to convince others. Doing your homework is the best way to formulate a plan. Learn what has and hasn't worked for other artists in the region. Products also have legal ramifications and descriptions and even liabilities.

THE IMAGE

Many entertainers don't think about their image but some have to. Major pop stars find a lot of money in marketing their image to third parties. The licensing to manufacturers of pop star action figures, posters, t-shirts, and other artist memorabilia can make up a significant portion of overall earnings. In many cases the artist's image is the driving force behind such merchandising. A super hottie pop star's bikini poster may be a hot seller—as long as the artist still looks hot—and some artists may spend a lot of time keeping that image. An artist's image is everything in the public venue and many artists are very concerned about how their image is marketed. They don't want bad photos circulating and may prohibit cameras at their concert appearances. Keeping a tight rein on product branding and image is a very important part of any campaign for wide public recognition and acceptance.

Some of the rights you may be negotiating will be specific to image—particularly video, film, and still photography. Your image may be a main component of your product so it is something always worth considering.

The casual weekend warrior may never have a need for any legality in their performance career. The warrior might have a day job and is only performing for the love of music and a little beer money. The band mates might all feel the same way. At the end of the night they split the money and go home. The entire arrangement is casual and friendly and aspirations are not that high. On the other hand, there are emerging bands that are dead serious about the business, their exposure, and careers. Let's move on to a more comprehensive view and see how deep the rabbit hole can go without ever leaving the garage.

CHAPTER 2

The Business of the Business

Jimmy Dale Gilmore, Courtesy of The Music Office

L et's get down to business by deciding when to get down to business. What are indicators that an informal and casual handshake might not suffice as the band goes forward? Here are a few road signs that might point in that direction:

▶ You are likely to receive IRS form 1099 from one or more employers.

▶ The act is earning over $10,000 a month.

▶ The act is performing before more than 2,000 people per month.

▶ The act is getting regional or national radio airplay.

▶ The act is garnering significant press.

Any of these indicators should tell you that a firm foundation for your band business is in order before the house collapses further down the road.

This chapter will guide you through the fundamentals of what constitutes an intellectual property and how these properties are conveyed and marketed to other business entities and the public. An entertainment business is bound by the same laws of business physics that affect all business—things like cash flow, depreciation, tax write-offs, and such. Like all small businesses, a music startup with a plan and a lot of hard work behind it can find success. The truth of the matter is that according to the Small Business Administration, statically most new small businesses fail and regardless of what sector of the economy the business is in, the top three reasons for failure are the same:

▶ Insufficient Startup Capital

This is where a band fund that pulls at least 10 percent off the top can come in handy. You can make a killer gig poster on your computer but you still have to have a few bucks on hand to make copies. Recording budgets can come from the same place. You don't need a million bucks to get started as in many businesses, but you need at least enough to get a promotional and recording ball rolling.

▶ Inadequate Business Planning and Marketing Plans

It all boils down to a plan. If you don't have one, sit down with a pen and piece of paper and jot one down. Start with 90 days. What do you want to accomplish in that time? Where does the band want to be one year from now in terms of earnings and exposure? What is the plan to get there? Is that plan realistic? "We kick ass for a year and blow them all away" is not a plan but a dream. Learn to tell the difference.

▶ Unrealistic Accounting and Cash Flow Projections (Blue Sky)

In business, when rosy business plans or startup pro formas are being put forward they generally will contain what is known as "blue sky." This is overvaluing the assets or the business plan by using figures and projections that you pull out of the blue sky.

A recent partnership for a local club came by for some consulting and showed me a pro forma that would make money for all the investors in a short period of time. There were weekly, monthly, and quarterly sales projections that were plotted out for five years. When I asked the source of the projection data, I was told that it was the estimate of the General Partner. Who was the guy putting the deal together? The General Partner. The place went under in about 100 days and all the investors lost their shirts.

THE FOUNDATION OF IT ALL—THE COPYRIGHT

The copyright is the core basis of any artistic endeavor and drives the entire entertainment industry. Most of the paperwork in the business is the assignment and licensing of copyrights; most commonly CDs, DVDs, film and videos, distribution, and streaming rights between two parties. A copyright is much the same as a patent for an invention or process. It is a claim of ownership and exclusive rights to the property that is the foundation of any license or copyright enforcement claim. Here are a few frequently asked questions regarding copyrights:

How Do I Copyright a Song?

Copyrighting a song is a pretty straight forward process. You merely state your claim of ownership in authoring/writing the piece. On a copy of a song you composed you could affix the "©" copyright symbol and it has been copyrighted—at least in your mind and notebook. Legally it's yours. On the other hand, you may want to declare to more than just yourself that you own the piece.

In the case of infringement where the origin of the song is the point being argued in court, the party who can show the earliest claim of ownership will usually prevail. If someone copyrights a song in 2006 and the other party copyrighted the song in 1994 and can prove it, the earlier date is the first date of the rights being claimed. Bottom line: the issue with a copyright claim is not so much who as when.

Why Should I Register My Copyright with the Library Of Congress?

The most common way and an absolute necessity if a song is likely to actually be bought, sold, or licensed is to have the creative property claim registered with the United States Library of Congress. This registry acts as the legal timestamp of an authorship and ownership claim. The Library of Congress currently charges $45 to timestamp your claim of ownership. Before sending in your application, it is a good idea to make sure the rate hasn't gone up by visiting www.copyright.gov for any changes in pricing. There are different forms for different copyrights but the primary tools for the music industry will be Form PA and Form SR. We will look at these two forms in some detail.

Keep in mind that copyrighting a song does not indemnify you from infringement claims. Contrary to urban legend, the Library of Congress doesn't listen to all the music submitted. I would be surprised if they even confirmed that there actually was a song on the CD or tape. They are merely acting as the registrar/timestamp for a claim of ownership.

When you hear a song on the radio, there are actually two copyrights that are usually in play. The first copyright is the copyright that is owned by the songwriter or composer. This copyright owner granted to the artist performing the song the right to perform it. The artist or their label also owns the copyright for the actual recording that is made. The song has two parts: the composer/creator and the performer. If someone else wanted to cover the song, they would need the permission of the copyright owner of the song. If someone wanted to use, for example, an artist's recording on a film soundtrack, they would need the permission of both the writer and the label or artist that owns the performance.

How Long Does a Copyright Last?

At the time of this writing, (and the major labels are now lobbying to extend copyright terms into centuries), a copyright will last the life of the composer/author plus seventy-five years. A song recorded today by a 20-year-old young gun may not see the light of public domain until sometime after 2150. I guess the short answer is "a long time."

Do I Have To Write Notated Music To Copyright a Song?

No. Library of Congress now accepts CDs and cassettes. See the instructions on copyright forms below. The form with full instructions is also on the CD-ROM.

Is There an Alternative To Paying So Much For a Copyright?

For the starting songwriter, especially the prolific, copyrighting every single song through the Library of Congress can be an expensive proposition. Luckily, there is a perfectly legal way around spending $45 every time you come up with a good hook. Copyright a number of songs under one title. "Songscapes of John Songwriter, Vol. 1" will timestamp the entire collection and one of the component songs can be later culled from the herd and copyrighted again.

Another commonly used method is the "poor man's copyright" using the U.S. Postal Service. Send a CD of the music, along with a lyric sheet to yourself via registered mail. Do not open the package. The package has the timestamp from the post office and could be entered into evidence in court later if necessary. I find this the least desirable method of protection as it offers you the least. We'll start with a more in-depth look at the two most common and important copyright forms, Form PA and Form SR.

Let's take a quick look at Form PA, the best legal foundation for a copyright claim. All the forms mentioned in this chapter and throughout the book are on the accompanying CD-ROM with detailed instructions. See What's On the CD-ROM for a complete listing of the forms.

FORM PA

This is the form you will use to copyright a single song or collection of songs with the Library of Congress. Again, the form is on the CD-ROM and we will just look at a few of the more important parts.

TYPE OR PRINT IN BLACK INK. DO NOT WRITE ABOVE THIS LINE.		Correspondence Fee Received

Title of This Work: Alternative title or title of larger work in which this work was published:	**1**	
Name and Address of Author and Owner of the Copyright: Nationality or domicile: Phone, fax, and email:	**2**	Phone ( ) Fax ( ) Email:
Year of Creation:	**3**	
If work has been published, **Date and Nation of Publication:**	**4**	a. Date _____ *(Month, day, and year all required)* Month Day Year b. Nation
Type of Authorship in This Work: Check all that this author created.	**5**	❏ Music ❏ Other text (includes dramas, screenplays, etc.) ❏ Lyrics *(If your work is a motion picture or other audiovisual work, use the standard Form PA.)*
Signature: (Registration cannot be completed without a signature.)	**6**	*I certify that the statements made by me in this application are correct to the best of my knowledge.* Check one: ❏ Author ❏ Authorized agent X_____
OPTIONAL **Name and Address of Person to Contact for Rights and Permissions:** Phone, fax, and email:	**7**	❏ Check here if same as #2 above. Phone ( ) Fax ( ) Email:

Section one has one component that deserves comment. Remember a page or two back where we discussed copyrighting a collection of songs as one? When culling out a song for a previous, separate, stand-alone copyright, enter the originating title of the first copyright.

Example: "I Love My Baby"
Originally copyrighted as part of
"Songscapes of John Songwriter, Vol. 1"
LOC # ABCD-1234, May 2008

Section two is very important. Use your full legal name rather than a stage or entertainment name. Since it can take up to one year to have the copyright form returned to you, use the most permanent address you can come up with in a twenty-first century migrating society. When I was young, I used my parents' address because mine would change frequently. I now have a post office box as a permanent business address. In legal terms regarding the song, this is the owner and address of the copyright. It is assignable only by this person.

The rest of Form PA is pretty straight forward. If you wrote both the lyrics and music, tick both boxes. Enter a publisher name only if the song has been officially assigned to a publisher. For legal intents and purposes, a song is generally viewed as published only after the public has access to it.

The certificate mailing address is where they will send the document. Again, use a permanent address.

Be sure to sign the application and mail it to Library of Congress with a check or money order. I prefer a check as I get to see when I enter the queue at Library of Congress when the check clears. Be patient; it will be months before the document returns.

When you receive the form back from the Library of Congress, it will have a stamp on it in the upper right corner that will be the official and legal description of the song as an intellectual property. If you are assigning the rights to this song at a later time, you can use this legal description in the license agreement.

FORM SR

Now that we have the song covered, let's take a look at copyrighting the recording of that song using Form SR. Form SR is much the same as Form PA, but a bit more complex and with more variables.

Section one is much the same as Form PA and you can see that a space has been created in this form for inclusion of a derivative work or previous copyright.

Section two leaves room for more authors (something woefully missing in Form PA) and wants to know more about them.

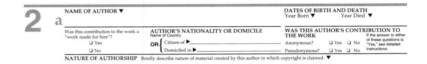

Sometimes the estate of a copyright owner will become the copyright claimant after the passing of the writer. Unless you are the executor or trustee of the writer's estate, leave this space blank.

That sums up our look at the basics of copyrights and the two most common and important copyright forms. The CD-ROM contains a number of other copyright forms for a number of scenarios such as a reassignment of copyright or an extension of the copyright period. Please keep in mind that the Library of Congress forms are up to date as of the time of this writing, but you may go online at copyright.com and download the latest forms. Now let's examine some other basic legal concepts that can have important implications regarding your future as an artist.

OTHER FUNDAMENTAL AND IMPORTANT CONCEPTS

Assigning vs. Licensing. Now that you own the rights to a given song or recording through the copyright procedure, let's take a look at how we would exploit these new legal entities when walking into a deal.

It boils down to two concepts: assigning and licensing. Simply put, assigning rights to your music is handing over the copyrights to that recording or song. Once assigned, it is completely out of your control. You are no longer the owner of that property. Your new partner will pay you a percentage or per-unit royalty for what sells, but they will make all the decisions regarding exploiting the property, accounting for the property, and re-assigning or licensing those rights to other third parties. You are completely out of the administrative loop. This is most commonly found in publishing agreements over song rights and recording deals over record rights. The publisher is the copyright holder and is in a revenue-sharing partnership with you. The publisher doesn't just take the money; they are responsible for all exploitation of the piece and the enforcement of its copyright. Many artists from unknowns to megastars have publishers handle this part of their career because unless the writer is a prolific author of hit material, it is easier to have a publisher handle all the administrative and marketing tasks.

A similar situation arises when an artist is signed to a label. When the CD is released, the product is owned completely by the record label, not the artist or the writers. All aspects of exploiting the recording are the label's responsibility and consequently they make all the calls.

The alternative to assigning the rights is to license them. This will give the licensee the rights to use, not own, the intellectual property for a given period of time for a specific amount; again, usually royalty based.

When an artist or their management licenses a product, it gives the buyer the right to manufacture, market, and sell products based on the artist and their image. An artist can license their logo to promote a beer or soft drink. An action figure manufacturer might want to license the rights to a successful artist. Regardless of how much money changes hands or what property is being conveyed, the important difference in licensing is that the license will expire at some time in the future. One of a successful manager's core duties is to license the brand to as many possible outlets as possible for the best price that can be obtained.

Another upside to licensing is it can be used as an incentive to the licensee to perform. If you own the material forever, you have no immediate compulsion to recoup your money immediately; you might save that great song in the catalog for the next hot artist you sign that needs a strong repertoire rather than just throwing it out to whoever will cut it. In the case of a license, the meter is running, the clock is ticking, and the licensee can only exploit and profit from the license for its term. It is a good incentive to get things done. I also view it as much easier to recapture your rights via reversion or litigation if it is a license you are trying to revoke rather than a copyright you are trying to recapture. Keep an eye out for this concept in the contract; assignments have been known to go by many names, but in the case of a license there will always be a stipulation for when the license and agreement expire. If there is no such wording, you are probably looking at an assignment in disguise. Cyclical wording can also be used to mask an assignment. In one paragraph, perhaps stuck in the definitions preamble to a contract, the term can be defined as the life of the copyright—a sure red flag for an assignment. Later in the document no further mention is made of any term to the agreement; all later clauses refer to the previous and more obscure definition. "As specified herein," "in compliance with the terms of this agreement," or "co-terminus with the license granted herein," can all be road signs to something sinister. Read those clauses at least twice and hunt down and understand the reference.

In every case possible, regarding every aspect of your career and image, license if you can and assign only if you must.

Reversion. Record labels and publishers regard this as the "R" word. Reversion means that the rights revert to the artist or writer for whatever reason. The primary use of reversion clauses in contracts is to gain leverage regarding the performance of the contract. A manager is granted exclusive rights to manage and market the band, but should the manager fall short of what was contractually expected, the rights can revert to the artist. Similar clauses are in almost all contracts granting rights to intellectual properties. If the buyer does not pay royalties on time or in the agreed amount, if the buyer doesn't hit certain legally-defined benchmarks, the rights they had will revert to the artist or their management.

You can even find reversion clauses in recording deals on occasion—almost always from a band with negotiating strength.

Especially regarding small and independent labels, a reversion clause is a necessity. Small and startup labels can go the extra distance for their artists; they sweat blood and put their hearts and souls into the enterprise, working untiringly for the music and artist. And, they typically go broke. Any deal with a small indie should include reversion rights for the artist that kick in as soon as the label's phone gets turned off.

Your Name. In most cases as a solo artist, your name is the brand for your product. Many artists come up with a stage name that might be snappier and easy to market than their given name. It might be easier to sell Johnny Slash than Jonathon Weisleschmadt, Jr. Another instance, when the given name or surname is common, it has already been used by another performer or artist. If your name is Nora Jones or Cher, you will be facing branding and recognition problems if you go forward trying to use your birth name.

I was talking to a friend of mine not long ago and she was telling me about another friend and performer, (let's call her Lynn Morris) who was having trouble with her Internet presence because of another performer with the same name had already snagged the Website name. In this case, the late comer to the game actually changed her stage name to Linda Morris. That is a pretty radical solution, but the Internet, like so much of other parts of the business, is registered on a "first come, first served" basis.

A band name also serves as a trademark. You won't get very far, except to the nearest courtroom if you use a band name that is already taken. The odds of your band ZZ Top, prevailing against the Texas trio in court are slim to none. Many bands come up with a great name. Unfortunately it is someone else's. We will look at other legal implications regarding branding, including a sad tale of an Austin band as we progress.

Your Acumen. Have you ever watched a family fight over the estate of a dearly departed? Even though they are blood kin, they battle against each other ruthlessly when it comes down to Grandpa Jones' estate. It can get nasty. The more comprehensive the will, the less controversy will come to light. The breakup of a band can be similar. Band mates and friends for years can get into heated and contentious arguments over money. When you are starting out and there is no money to argue about, it is not much of an issue, but should success find its way to your doorstep, like the family fighting over an estate, even the best of friends and band mates can become adversaries when a bit of money is the object of contention.

Taking care of business is just that. If you think the band is starting to grow legs and is moving toward public recognition and increased earnings, it is not a bad idea to get the band together and talk about the legal and monetary basis on which the band is going to go forward. Foundations are poured at the beginning of any construction project, not the end. Now is the time to start building and it is much easier early on; you can get a handle on how everyone views the business of the band. The artistic personality may have an aversion to taking care of business, but you will only be more empowered and in a stronger negotiating position if you have some concept of what is being defined.

Talent can get you a hearing and maybe even a deal, but only business acumen will sustain your career. Ever wonder why a lot of one-hit-wonders are living in trailer parks today and some on the beach in Malibu? Talent has nothing to do with these different results. As previously mentioned, artists get screwed in writing. Can the label really be blamed when the artist comes to the table a clueless rube and leaves broke? Is it the label's fault that the band came into the deal unarmed and naked?

Let's revisit the Today Tones for a band meeting about a year after their formation.

Part II

Teaming Up

CHAPTER 3

Collaborating and Joining Forces

Jesse Taylor, Courtesy of The Music Office

"Under God, all are created equal but record labels use another formula."

After a year together, the Today Tones have been getting their chops up and are playing more gigs each month. The band is moving toward an original show, replacing their older repertoire of cover tunes with songs written by band members. There is a regional buzz around the band and it's time to get down to work and work out how Today Tones is going to handle the business of the business.

It is becoming increasingly apparent that the band is going to need a few legal entities to move forward. The band now has a Website and wants to sell CDs and other merchandise. The band has had a couple double-booking incidents because all the band members were soliciting gigs and sometimes stepped on each other's scheduling toes. The band will need one point of contact from here forward. There are monthly band expenses starting to accrue: the Website fees, the recurring ad in a local entertainment weekly, and other regular expenses. Just as there needs to be one point of contact, there needs to be one place the band earnings are funneled in and out of—the band bank account.

THE BRAND NAME

As discussed in a previous chapter, the band name is what brands the product. It would be a good idea to get on the Internet and Google around to see if any other band has already taken the name you want to use. Also, search some of the big CD/DVD sites like Amazon to see if anyone with your name is selling product.

Creating a trademark comes to mind when securing a name or logo, but in the case of a band or artist, there is another place to start. A trademark is defined as a word, phrase, design, symbol, or other device that labels the product and sets it apart from other products. A physical product is what we are talking about in this case. A band or artist is more accurately providing a service which makes the service mark more applicable to defending the brand. At a later time, when the "Today Tones Action Figure" actually becomes a physical product is when you would trademark the brand.

You cannot use a service or trademark that has been taken—again, even in some cases if it is your surname. Don't plan on calling your band, "Dillards," or "McDonalds." You would also have a hard time acquiring a trademark for the name of your band, "The Lowes." Even changing it to, "The Home Despots" might get you in some trouble with a humorless law firm.

In the 1980s, there was a popular band, Zeitgeist, from Austin, Texas that had built a large following and fan base. They were touring nationally and had just secured a deal with a major label. The only problem was that there was another musical group in Ohio that had already been using the name for over a decade. The Austin-based Zeitgeist soon became The Reivers after a cease and desist notice from the Ohio band's legal counsel. Needless to say this caused a lot of branding problems for the band who after reaching national recognition had to change their name, posters, stationery, business cards, and every other form of promotion, branding, and identity.

What this reflected is that the band didn't check to see if the name had already been taken. I feel that the Austin band probably could have prevailed as they had been touring nationally and there was no confusion, at least outside of Ohio, over which band was which. Many courts have found that two non-competing businesses, even of a like nature, that are separated by geographic distance can use the same trade name without damage being caused to either party. Perhaps the litigation necessary to prevail would have put things on hold for too long. If I was a record label executive that just signed a new act and the first order of business was to defend an infringement lawsuit, I would be less than enamored with the newly signed band and the delays it could mean.

Once the band has done its due diligence on a band name search and decided on a name, let's look at the role of each member of the band in terms of how we put a partnership together that will compensate everyone as fairly as possible. We will look at business and legal entities from the simplest to the more complex.

THE MEMBERS

Every member of the band brings something to the table. Each member of the band values their own talents and contribution as much as any other member.

The Today Tones have four members who all play instruments, but Jim the lead singer/front man also writes all of the band's original material. To date, the band income and expenses have been shared equally and that is the plan for the immediate future. It is necessary for the band to become a legal entity. In this case, we will use a simple general partnership to get the ball rolling.

A general partnership, second only to a sole proprietorship, is the simplest and least expensive method to create a business entity. The terms can be plain and simple, and easily understood by all the band members. Here is an outline of the salient points that could be covered in this simple agreement. One of the band members should be selected to be the point of contact. All communications should flow through one person. The decisions can be made by all, but if one person acts as the traffic cop, much less will fall between the cracks.

There are pitfalls to a general partnership you should be aware of. All the partners in the partnership are equally and severally responsible for band liabilities. This means that members of the partnership could be *sued as individuals.* There is no layer of liability protection that you might find in other more complex vehicles like limited partnerships, sub S corporations, limited liability companies and the like. We will be looking more closely at those platforms shortly. Simplicity can have its costs.

THE BAND/ARTIST ASSETS

There are two components to the asset list of an artist or band; the intellectual properties or "soft" assets, and the physical property or "hard" assets of the band such as equipment or vehicles. Generally speaking, when you are putting together a band-as-a-business you will be listing at least the following assets:

▶ Band Name and Logo

▶ The right to make decisions and enter into agreements, conduct business legally

▶ Original Song Compositions

▶ Original Sound Recordings

▶ Performance Income

▶ Artist/Band Image

▶ Merchandising Income

▶ Sponsorship Income

▶ Endorsement Income

▶ Physical Assets (equipment, vehicles, etc.)

These are the assets and rights you have been dealt at the beginning of your career. Their valuation is up to you. The parts are inter-dependent; you will not get an endorsement offer before a live performance or recording deal. Regardless of who you will be sitting down to negotiate with, you will be selling the above items. Your goal as an artist or manager is to make relinquishing these rights expensive for the purchaser and the purchaser wants everything on the menu at the lowest possible cost.

SONGWRITING ROYALTIES CONCERNS

Let's talk about Jim, the songwriter in the band, for a moment. The songs are actually Jim's property and not the band's. This has been a point of contention for many band members in the past when they discover that they don't share in writer royalties. For purposes of the band's partnership, songwriting royalties are off the table as a shared asset. Some bands will compose all their material together and all should be credited and compensated as writers. They are songwriting as a team.

EQUIPMENT AND OTHER HARD ASSET CONCERNS

Does the band own the equipment or does each member contribute what they can? Equipment brought to the table by each member should be regarded as the property of that member; not a contribution to the band's assets. Equipment that is later purchased by the band, in many cases a PA system, is an asset owned by the band and each partner in this scenario owns 25 percent. If a member leaves the band, the remaining band members should pay to the exiting member his or her share of the market value of equipment purchased while in the band. The remaining original members now own the PA system three ways. When a new member joins the band, he only shares a percentage of the equipment purchased since coming aboard. Can you see how convoluted the accounting can get when, for example, after a few years a six-piece band is down to two original members and has new members who have been in for different lengths of time? This scenario can change as a group finds success. In many cases a longtime band member who has left will still share in some band revenue such as CD sales and merchandising of products using the ex-member's image manufactured during his or her tenure.

We will look at the sole proprietor one-man-band scenario a bit later but for now let's look at how a group might approach cutting up the pie. The first deal you will need to cut is with your band mates. In most casual situations a hand shake is enough for weekend warriors, but when a group is serious about creating and branding a new sound and image, it is a good idea to get down the rules of the road between the band early on. It is time to think of your band partners as partners in a legal sense.

CHAPTER 4

The Band Business Foundation

Duluth, Courtesy of The Music Office

The time has arrived to look at legal concepts that are close to home. We now understand that when boiled down to its basics, we are creating copyrights that we are going to sell. These copyrights may be fortunate enough to have considerable cash value at some time in the future. We now need to address how we are going to split up that cash when it comes through the door.

Sharing Percentages among Partners. The first thing is to define what is being shared by whom and in what percentages. Here's an excerpt from the more comprehensive General Partnership Agreement on the CD-ROM.

Profits and Losses. *Until modified by mutual consent of all the Partners, the profits and losses of the Partnership and all items of income, gain, loss, deduction, or credit shall be shared by the Partners in the following proportions:*

Partner	Share in Profit and Loss
Jim Halbertson	25%
Bob Dobbs	25%
Jack Benimble	25%
Sam Jackson	25%

The above is a pretty simple statement but there could be other considerations. Take a look at the variety of partnerships, LLCs and other contracts on the CD-ROM. The waters of corporate legal matters can get very murky very quickly and it is advisable to have competent counsel review any deals you're considering.

Let's take a look at a chart of how a band might view their relationship before entering into a general partnership or other legal entity (see page 35–36). There is a copy of the form on the CD-ROM that you can customize.

In a few paragraphs and filling out one form, we can arrive at the basis for a simple partnership among band members. It is very simple and doesn't cover all of the complexities of the industry, but it will put a firm foundation under a good regional cover band that is pulling in some regular money. For bands performing original music and basing their income and success on the sale and performance of original music, things get much stickier and we will visit that scenario in a moment. For now let's look at a plain vanilla partnership agreement (see pages 37–41). It covers all the basics necessary to get the ball rolling and gives all the parties involved their legal due and piece of the action.

MUSIC BUSINESS CONTRACTS

BAND MEMBER SHARING PERCENTAGES WORKSHEET

BAND NAME: The Marvellettos

BAND MEMBERS   **Name**   **Title**
       Example   John Doe   Drums

ASSET	SHARING PERCENTAGE
Name of Band, Logo and Service Mark	Shared equally by all band members.
Right to be a Contract Signatory	Shared equally by all members with Billy acting as band spokesman and signatory. A majority of band members must approve all deals involving over $250.
Rights to Writer Royalties	The writers of the songs retain all songwriting credits and copyrights. Non-writer members do not share in this income.
Rights to Sound Recordings	Shared equally by all band members.
Rights to Accounting	A bookkeeper or accountant will be elected by a majority of the band to handle the group's accounting. All members have access to these records and books.
Rights to Performance Income	Shared equally by all band members.
Rights to Merchandising Income	Shared equally by all band members.
Rights to Outside Income (endorsements)	Shared equally by all band members except in the case of a product being endorsed by a member as an individual. The band will not share in a member's individual third party income.
Physical & Hard Assets of the Band	The ownership of all equipment paid for by the band is to be shared equally by all band members. Items that are owned and paid for by individual members are the property of that member.
Right to Expel a Member	A band member can be expelled by the majority vote of the other members. The member to be expelled has no vote.

BandWorksheet

Rights of an Exiting Member

Expelled members or those that leave the band of their own volition shall share in that portion of the assets that were acquired while a member. The physical assets of the group acquired during this period shall be assigned a fair market value and the exiting member shall be paid their share.

In the case of ongoing merchandise or sales of recordings, the exiting band member shall retain their share, if any, that they had as a member until such physical inventory is reduced to zero.

Rights to Add a New Member or Guest

A band member may be hired only upon the unanimous agreement of the band. A support musician may be hired on a temporary basis and work-for-hire basis by the majority agreement of the band members.

Rights of a New Band Member

A new member shall receive a full member share of performance income but shall share in one-half share of any other income produced by the band for a period of one year. After one year, the member shall be viewed as fully vested in the band and shall receive a full band member share from that time forward.

In the Event of a Vote Tie

In the event of a tie vote that requires a majority of the band, the band member previously selected to be the band spokesman shall have the tie-breaking vote. In the event that the issue being voted on is about the band spokesman, lots shall be drawn between the other members to decide who has the tie-breaking vote.

Disbanding

If the group completely disbands and ceases business permanently, all assets held by the band shall be liquidated at fair market value and the proceeds shall be distributed to band members in accordance with their sharing percentages.

General Partnership Agreement

This Partnership Agreement ("Agreement") made and effective this [Date], by and between the following individuals, referred to in this Agreement as the "Partners":

Partners Names:
Jim Halbertson
Robert Dobbs
Jack Benimble
Sam Jackson

The Partners wish to set forth, in a written agreement, the terms and conditions by which they will associate themselves in the Partnership.

Now, therefore, in consideration of the promises contained in this Agreement, the Partners affirm in writing their association as a partnership in accordance with the following provisions:

1. Name and Place of Business. The name of the partnership shall be called Acme Music Management Co. (the "Partnership"). Its principal place of business shall be:

1234 S. Main St.
Suite 9876
Somewhereville, CA 98765

until changed by agreement of the Partners, but the Partnership may own property and transact business in any and all other places as may from time to time be agreed upon by the Partners.

2. Purpose. The purpose of the Partnership shall be to [Business Description]. The Partnership may also engage in any and every other kind or type of business, whether or not pertaining to the foregoing, upon which the Partners may at any time or from time to time agree.

3. Term. The Partnership shall commence as of the date of this Agreement and shall continue until terminated as provided herein.

4. Capital Accounts. The Partners shall make an initial investment of capital, contemporaneously with the execution of this Agreement, as follows:

Partner	Contribution
Jim Halbertson	$50,000
Robert Dobbs	$20,000
Jack Benimble	$15,000
Sam Jackson	$15,000

In addition to each Partner's share of the profits and losses of the Partnership, as set forth in Section 5, each Partner is entitled to an interest in the assets of the Partnership.

The amount credited to the capital account of the Partners at any time shall be such amount as set forth in this Section 4 above, plus the Partner's share of the net profits of the Partnership and any additional capital contributions made by the Partner and minus the Partner's share of the losses of the Partnership and any distributions to or withdrawals made by the Partner. For all purposes of this Agreement, the Partnership net profits and each Partner's capital account shall be computed in accordance with generally accepted accounting principles, consistently applied, and each Partner's capital account, as reflected on the Partnership federal income tax return as of the end of any year, shall be deemed conclusively correct for all purposes, unless an objection in writing is made by any Partner and delivered to the accountant or accounting firm preparing the income tax return within one (1) year after the same has been filed with the Internal Revenue Service. If an objection is so filed, the validity of the objection shall be conclusively determined by an independent certified public accountant or accounting firm mutually acceptable to the Partners.

5. Profits and Losses. Until modified by mutual consent of all the Partners, the profits and losses of the Partnership and all items of income, gain, loss, deduction, or credit shall be shared by the Partners in the following proportions:

Partner	Share in Profit and Loss
Jim Halbertson	50%
Robert Dobbs	20%
Jack Benimble	15%
Sam Jackson	15%

6. Books and Records of Account. The Partnership books and records shall be maintained at the principal office of the Partnership and each Partner shall have access to the books and records at all reasonable times.

7. Future Projects. The Partners recognize that future projects for the Partnership depend upon many factors beyond present control, but the Partners wish to set forth in writing and to mutually acknowledge their joint understanding, intentions, and expectations that the relationship among the Partners will continue to flourish in future projects on similar terms and conditions as set forth in this Agreement, but there shall be no legal obligations among the Partners to so continue such relationship in connection with future projects.

8. Time and Salary. Until and unless otherwise decided by unanimous agreement of the Partners, **Martin A. Smith** shall act as Managing Partner and shall be empowered to conduct the day-to-day business of the Partnership. Each Partner shall nonetheless be expected to devote such time and attention to Partnership affairs as shall from time to time be determined by agreement of the Partners. No Partner shall be entitled to any salary or to any compensation for services rendered to the Partnership or to another Partner.

9. Transfer of Partnership Interests.
>   A. *Restrictions on Transfer*. None of the Partners shall sell, assign, transfer, mortgage, encumber, or otherwise dispose of the whole or part of that Partner's interest in the Partnership, and no purchaser or other transferee shall have any rights in the Partnership

as an assignee or otherwise with respect to all or any part of that Partnership interest attempted to be sold, assigned, transferred, mortgaged, encumbered, or otherwise disposed of, unless and to the extent that the remaining Partner(s) have given consent to such sale, assignment, transfer, mortgage, or encumbrance, but only if the transferee forthwith assumes and agrees to be bound by the provisions of this Agreement and to become a Partner for all purposes hereof, in which event, such transferee shall become a substituted partner under this Agreement.

B. *Transfer Does Not Dissolve Partnership.* No transfer of any interest in the Partnership, whether or not permitted under this Agreement, shall dissolve the Partnership. No transfer, except as permitted under Subsection 9.A. above, shall entitle the transferee, during the continuance of the Partnership, to participate in the management of the business or affairs of the Partnership, to require any information or account of Partnership transactions, or to inspect the books of account of the Partnership; but it shall merely entitle the transferee to receive the profits to which the assigning Partner would otherwise be entitled and, in case of dissolution of the Partnership, to receive the interest of the assigning Partner and to require an account from the date only of the last account agreed to by the Partners.

10. Death, Incompetency, Withdrawal, or Bankruptcy. Neither death, incompetency, withdrawal, nor bankruptcy of any of the Partners or of any successor in interest to any Partner shall operate to dissolve this Partnership, but this Partnership shall continue as set forth in Section 3, subject, however, to the following terms and conditions:

A. *Death or Incompetency.* In the event any Partner dies or is declared incompetent by a court of competent jurisdiction, the successors in interest of that Partner shall succeed to the partnership interest of that Partner and shall have the rights, duties, privileges, disabilities, and obligations with respect to this Partnership, the same as if the successors in interest were parties to this Agreement, including, but not limited to, the right of the successors to share in the profits or the burden to share in the losses of this Partnership, in the same manner and to the same extent as the deceased or incompetent Partner; the right of the successors in interest to continue in this Partnership and all such further rights and duties as are set forth in this Agreement with respect to the Partners, the same as if the words "or his or her successors in interest" followed each reference to a Partner; provided, however, that no successor in interest shall be obligated to devote any service to this Partnership and, provided further, that such successors in interest shall be treated as holding a passive, rather than active, ownership investment.

B. *Payments upon Retirement or Withdrawal of Partner.*
(1) Amount of Payments. Upon the retirement or withdrawal of a Partner, that Partner or, in the case of death or incompetency, that Partner's legal representative shall be entitled to receive the amount of the Partner's capital account (as of the end of the fiscal year of the Partnership next preceding the day on which the retirement or withdrawal occurs) adjusted for the following:

Page 3 of 5

(i) Any additional capital contributions made by the Partner and any distributions to or withdrawals made by the Partner during the period from the end of the preceding fiscal year to the day on which the retirement or withdrawal occurs;

(ii) The Partner's share of profits and losses of the Partnership from the end of the preceding fiscal year of the Partnership to the day on which the retirement or withdrawal occurs, determined in accordance with generally accepted accounting principles, consistently applied; and

(iii) The difference between the Partner's share of the book value of all of the Partnership assets and the fair market value of all Partnership assets, as determined by a fair market value appraisal of all assets. Unless the retiring or withdrawing Partner and the Partnership can agree on one appraiser, three (3) appraisers shall be appointed—one by the Partnership, one by the retiring or withdrawing Partner, and one by the two appraisers thus appointed. All appraisers shall be appointed within fifteen (15) days of the date of retirement or withdrawal. The average of the three appraisals shall be binding on all Partners.

(2) Time of Payments. Subject to a different agreement among the Partners or successors thereto, the amount specified above shall be paid in cash, in full, but without interest, no later than twelve (12) months following the date of the retirement or withdrawal.

(3) Alternate Procedure. In lieu of purchasing the interest of the retiring or withdrawing Partner as provided in subparagraph (1) and (2) above, the remaining Partners may elect to dissolve, liquidate and terminate the Partnership. Such election shall be made, if at all, within thirty (30) days following receipt of the appraisal referred to above.

11. Procedure on Dissolution of Partnership. Except as provided in Section 10.B.(3) above, this Partnership may be dissolved only by a unanimous agreement of the Partners. Upon dissolution, the Partners shall proceed with reasonable promptness to liquidate the Partnership business and assets and wind-up its business by selling all of the Partnership assets, paying all Partnership liabilities, and by distributing the balance, if any, to the Partners in accordance with their capital accounts, as computed after reflecting all losses or gains from such liquidation in accordance with each Partner's share of the net profits and losses as determined under Section 5.

12. Title to Partnership Property. If for purposes of confidentiality, title to Partnership property is taken in the name of a nominee or of any individual Partner, the assets shall be considered to be owned by the Partnership and all beneficial interests shall accrue to the Partners in the percentages set forth in this Agreement.

13. Leases. All leases of Partnership assets shall be in writing and on forms approved by all the Partners.

14. Controlling Law. This Agreement and the rights of the Partners under this Agreement shall be governed by the laws of the State of _____.

15. Notices. Any written notice required by this Agreement shall be sufficient if sent to the Partner or other party to be served by registered or certified mail, return receipt requested, addressed to the Partner or other party at the last known home or office address, in which event the date of the notice shall be the date of deposit in the United States mails, postage prepaid.

16. General. This Agreement contains the entire agreement of the Partners with respect to the Partnership and may be amended only by the written agreement executed and delivered by all of the Partners.

17. Binding upon Heirs. This Agreement shall bind each of the Partners and shall inure to the benefit of (subject to the Sections 9 and 10) and be binding upon their respective heirs, executors, administrators, devisees, legatees, successors and assigns.

In Witness Whereof, the Partners have executed this Agreement the date first above written.

_____   _____
Partner   Partner

_____   _____
Partner   Partner

Page 5 of 5

GENERAL PARTNERSHIP AGREEMENT

There is very little to comment on this contract as it is neat and tidy. The largest equity partner will be acting as general manager of the partnership until it is decided otherwise by the remaining partners. This partnership is totally plain vanilla and could be used for an auto parts store as easily as a music company. A general partnership is a good place to start, and, if the partners are in agreement, relatively easily transformed into a limited partnership, LLC, sub S or C corporation at a later date if the business grows or another round of investment needs to be sought out.

The most important thing to consider when joining into a general partnership is that there is no layer of liability protection for the partners. If the partnership gets sued and the assets of the partnership are inadequate to cover the judgment, the prevailing party can blow right through the partnership to the personal assets of the partners. This is why general partnerships are often modified to other business types within months of the initial formation. A structure is in place to start conducting business, but hopefully liability protection will come into play before the enterprise grows large enough to be viewed as target for litigation.

OTHER BUSINESS PLATFORMS

The general partnership is great for sorting out who shares in what. But, what will occur when a key member exits, for example the general manager in the above deal? There are other ways to skin this cat that are much more comprehensive and consequently expensive. A formative general partnership may serve to cover some bases early on, but it is the more formal and consequently more expensive business types that afford liability protection to the participants. Let's take a look at the most common and see some of their strengths and weaknesses.

The Limited Partnership

This is a common vehicle for a new business startup. The limited partners own a percentage of the business but have no direct say in the day-to-day business. The limited partners have a layer of liability protection as most lawsuits will not blow through the partnership to the limited partners. One of the reasons that limited partnerships are showing a downturn in popularity is that business losses don't pass through to the partners. If the business has ten investors and loses $100,000 in a given year, the business gets a write off for the bad year but the write offs don't pass through directly to the investors. This change was made in the late 1980s and has slowed the injection of cash to small businesses and startups. If your rich Uncle Bob invested in you and lost, he could write it off in those days.

The LLC

This is very similar to a limited partnership and is described by some as the best of both a partnership and a corporation. The LLC offers tax advantages and liability protection for the members. Generally speaking each member's personal liability is limited to the amount of their investment. If an LLC only has one partner, the IRS will view it as identical to a sole proprietorship. Members will also be taxed as if partners with profits and losses flowing through to the member's tax returns directly. An LLC will also allow for foreign investment where general or C corporate structures generally require U.S. citizenship or residence to participate. LLCs have accounting hoops you must jump through but there is a more casual approach to other parts of administration. For example, no annual board meetings or corporate minutes are required. Last and not least, an LLC is not limited to the number of partners (investors) as some corporate models are. Some of the IRS forms common in LLC filings are Form 1065, K-1, and 1040 with Schedule E. Examples of these forms are on the CD-ROM.

Sub Chapter S Corporation

The tax status of an S corporation is similar to a limited partnership or LLC in that flow-through taxation is also a prime component of the platform. The stockholders in an S corp will show the profits or losses of the corporation on their individual tax filings. Like the other common corporate models, annual meetings and reporting to investors is quite formal and necessary.

Another limitation to a sub S corporation is that, for the most part, only individuals may participate. Not only is it limited to individuals, but the sub S is also limited to only 100 investors. There is some room in the law for the participation of some trusts or other entities that act as individuals, but investment by another corporation or business is not allowed. Like the C corporation, all allocation of dividends or other assets of the company are in direct proportion to the amount of stock being held by the individual investors. The more stock owned by an investor, the stronger their voice in management.

C Corporation

A C or general corporation is probably the most common vehicle found in medium to large enterprises. One of the major down sides to a C corporation is that it can result in "double taxation" for the stockholders. The corporation first pays taxes at the corporate level on net income. Should dividends be paid to stockholders, they in turn will have to declare this income on their individual returns.

Another aspect of the C corporation is that distributions to shareholders must be in proportion to the number of shares they hold. This makes a C corporation a bit more democratic in terms of stockholder equity. At the end of the day, the stockholders in a C corporation call the shots, and if they are unhappy, an election to change management or policies can be called by members at the annual meeting.

Everyone views things through the lens of their own bias. Greed is not unique to the music industry. When making business and legal decisions within the band or with outside third parties, everyone at the table has their own personal agenda that will have to be addressed during negotiations. The secret to a successful deal is to balance all these agendas into a compromise that will work best for all the parties involved. Stalemates occur, sometimes to the point of killing the deal, but negotiating honestly and in good faith early on can take you further down the road and faster.

If I was the Today Tones drummer, who didn't write any songs for the group, I might look at it like this: There are five members in the band. If we are to share equally in the band's success and we don't add or remove any members, we should each receive twenty percent of the band's income.

If I was the lead singer, who is the primary writer in the band, I might have a slightly different outlook: I'm the core figure in the band's image; I'm the front man and I write the songs. I should be paid as two people. That would mean we cut the pie six ways where I get two shares and the other members get one. Of course, I would keep all the writer/publisher rights to all my songs.

The bass player has a simple formula in mind: There are five of us. Split five ways, that's twenty percent each. The rhythm section has to stick together.

None of these scenarios are realistic. A great deal more thought will have to go into the sharing percentages of the band's income and assets. Our previous worksheet might fall short of what really needs to be spelled out; thus the need for something more comprehensive than a simple partnership or sole proprietorship. We will need to start working our way toward hooking up with a label or management, but first, let's look at a startup check list that will help move things forward.

CHAPTER 5

Putting It All Together

Kathy Matea and Greg Forest, Courtesy of The Music Office

A successful music career is made up of a number of components and many of them—demos, Websites, and such—are not options but vital necessities. Let's take a look at some of the things we can do to cement our foundation together.

Get a Post Office Box. Now that the Today Tones partnership is up and running, at least on a piece of paper, get a post office box for the partnership.

File a DBA. Once you have a partnership underway, it needs to have a legal name and the easiest way to get started is to go down to your local courthouse and file a DBA (Doing Business As) or fictitious name certificate. The Today Tones Partnership would register itself as the owner of the business doing business as the Today Tones. Use the post office box as the business address and the designated band leader as the phone or other information.

Open a Bank Account. A great deal of the day-to-day business you conduct is likely to occur over the Internet. That will require a bank account and credit or debit card—the next step in creating your legal and business bona fides. Open a band checking account and take a percentage off the top of each gig to plant a little security. This asset is also shared equally by all members of the group and an exiting member would get their share. Get a debit card for the account that you can use for band purchases and road emergencies. I recommend going with a national chain as making deposits on the road is far smarter and safer than touring with a suitcase full of cash. Cash deposits are usually credited to the account the same day and will increase the buying power of your debit card immediately. A credit card at this point is probably not a good idea as it further complicates matters when a band member exits with a possible credit card balance owed. The band should want to build a financial war chest—not a pile of debt.

Make a Band Demo. Try to get a good demo together as soon as possible. You don't have to make it a full blown CD production, but merely a good sonic example of what the band really sounds like. An overblown production can actually hurt you in this scenario. Club owners can do math. When they hear a band demo with a horn section or five backup vocals when the band is only a trio, they know that the CD is no reflection of the band's live ability. If you're courageous enough, shop a live recording.

I feel it is very important whether the recording is just a demo or a finished master to digitally sign it in every case. When a song is rendered digitally it can contain more than just the audio performance. Embedded in the file, whether on CD or in an MP3, can be copyright information, song title and artist, even a picture in some cases. If you don't know how to do this, ask your engineer to do it for you. This procedure brands the file as yours. No matter how many copies are ripped and how far it is distributed it is like having a watermark on the performance. Your demo could end up places you never intended it to go and it could come back to bite you later.

In 1984, I was asked to play guitar for the twentieth reunion concert of the 13th Floor Elevators. They were a band I had a lot of respect for and I considered it an honor to take the place of the guitarist, Stacy Sutherland, who had died five years earlier. Two years later, John Ike Walton, the drummer called me and asked if I had heard the CD yet. What CD? Some bozo in the third row had recorded the show on a jam box and licensed the recording to one of the biggest rip off record companies in the world—Collectable Records.

I ordered a CD from their Website immediately and waited with guns loaded for the CD to be delivered confirming the theft. A few days later the CD arrived and before playing it I looked at the credits and the songs were listed, but none of the band members were even mentioned. I was getting furious by this time. They had not only ripped off my performance, but gave me no credit for being a player. I popped the CD in my player.

Five minutes later I was thanking God that my name wasn't on the CD. It was horrendous. I revisited Collectable's site and looked through their catalog. I saw a lot of my friends in there also. After a bit of research, I found that the company was selling old band demos under names like, "The Today Tones, the Early Years." In these days of digital branding, taking down an outfit like Collectable would be easier as the provenance of a digital recording can be ascertained. Heaven knows where Collectable got their recordings, but I would hazard a guess that in no case was it from the band or their label or management. Needless to say, Collectable Records doesn't pay a plug nickel to any of the artists on their label that I know of. Brand your demos!

Get a Band Photo. Early on, it may be out of the range of a starting band to afford a professional photographer. Everyone either owns a digital camera or knows someone who does. Get the group together and take the photos. A couple of tips are to make the background attractive (the urban brick wall look is passé) and keep it simple framing the group nicely without too much dead space around the group. Choose about five of the best, crop and touch them up in Photoshop and save two copies: one as CMYK color and one as grayscale. We will learn more about working with professional photographers in Chapter 12.

Spend a bit of money and get a business card and promo kit together. Use your new debit card to find a good Internet host and get a Website up. Money spent on attractive and compelling promotional material is always well spent. Even if you can't afford a gold-embossed business card, you might be able to afford four-color printing.

THE SOLO ARTIST SCENARIO

A solo artist has a different path to tread legally although the underlying foundation is the same. Instead of a general partnership, the artist would file his DBA as a sole proprietorship. Like the general partnership a sole proprietorship leaves the door open to personal liability should litigation arise. The sole proprietor owns the business lock, stock, and barrel. Band members are independent contractors and are paid accordingly. You can file a DBA as John R. Artist doing business as Johnny Artist and you have created a separate legal entity. You will probably still need the post office box and bank account to separate your business from your personal life. This separation becomes more important as your career progresses. For tax purposes it is advantageous to have your business completely separate from your personal finances. When money crosses over from your personal life to your business and vice versa it is known as co-mingling assets and a red flag for tax audits.

Federal Tax ID. Whether a band is working under a partnership, LLC, or other platform and even if you are a sole proprietorship, to regard yourself as real business you will need a Federal Tax ID number. This will come in handy when working with banks and some vendors. Early on, a sole proprietor can use their Social Security number just fine, but when things grow legs and the day-to-day management of the money and banking is turned over to a manager or label, it would be better to convey the change with a tax ID number rather than letting the management or label continue to operate under your Social Security number. This also guides you to towards accurate bookkeeping. In just a few months you will start saving every single receipt. Yes, record keeping is a hassle, but you don't know what a hassle is until the IRS contacts you and asks what your band has been doing for the last five years. *That* is a hassle!

The AFM (American Federation of Musicians). In some markets you may find that joining the union is a good idea. In some markets and venues you *must* be a union member to take the stage. The union can be a great ally in securing some long-term security for band members. There are insurance, credit union, and retirement programs available that use the union's economy of scale to get good rates for their members. A common mistake is to regard the AFM as a booking agency. The union will often send work to their members, but in my experience the criteria for being offered a gig from the union is based primarily on union seniority rather than talent or popularity.

If you are pursuing a career in classical or theatrical stage music, the sooner you join the union the better. In most markets it is the union that negotiates with the larger venues for the wages paid to the symphony and other large ensembles. The union can also help you cut your paperwork. The AFM booking agreement (on the CD-ROM) has evolved over the decades into one of the scariest contracts in the eyes of potential defaulters. A venue or other talent buyer that doesn't perform to the contract conditions can wind up on the nationally-printed defaulters' list. Being the AFM deadbeat of the month is not something a reputable venue would want hanging around their neck. The AFM can also be your friend when you're on the road. If something goes wrong, you can call in for help and it is usually forthcoming.

The IRS Form 1099. It is likely that any venue or business that pays your band more than $600 a year is going to be sending you an IRS Form 1099 declaring their payment to you. If the Today Tune Band receives 1099s, the band in turn will have to send out 1099s to the members to declare the income paid to them.

Insurance. There are few things more tragic than a band on the road has checked in to a hotel for the night only to wake in the morning one trailer full of equipment short. Insurance doesn't come to mind early on, but having your gear ripped off with no insurance will surely put a speed bump in your path to success.

If you are a member of the AFM, there are policies available that are very affordable. The AFM is not the only entity that insures musical and band equipment. Look on the Internet for others. The going rate at the time of this writing ran from $25-35 per $1,000 worth of equipment annually. If the policy is one that covers the whole band it is a 100 percent tax write off above the line.

Your homeowner's policy may also have coverage for a certain percentage of your property that is stolen from home. When I was ripped off once in Europe, I jumped through the hoops of filing a police report and when I returned home was overjoyed to find my homeowner's policy covered my musical instruments, "not for professional use," of course. They even accepted the police report in Italian.

WORKING WITH VENUES AND CLUBS

The first outside business sitation you will probably deal with as an artist is your first gig. You are now out of the garage or woodshed and in the real world. The time has come to put a real market dollar amount on your talents. Coming up with that figure on your first gig is usually easy: it is almost always little or no money. Your product is not market-proven coming out of the starting blocks, so your negotiating strength is nil.

When approaching your first venue or club owner, show a bit of moxie, but a touch of humble should always be on hand. Keep in mind that you need the gig more than the venue owner needs an unproven band. Club owners are pretty savvy customers; they know that you can hire an A-team studio band to cut a killer CD, and sound nothing like that on stage with your garage buddies. Be honest about where you are coming from and how you think you can help the club draw more customers and grow its reputation.

The Scenario

The Band: We want to play every Tuesday night and try to build a crowd. We will call it "Today Tones Tuesdays!" and start by getting all our friends to come out and see us. We will put up posters and try to get some local airplay for our self-released CD. We would like $300 each Tuesday until we can build it into better wages. Free drinks would be nice.

The Club: I've never heard of you. Lots of bands want to play here. I like your CD and your Tuesday idea might have some merit if you can draw. I will give you $150 for the first Tuesday and if it goes well, $200 for the one after that. If we are still talking to each other three months from now and you guys draw, you'll get your $300, but you have to prove yourselves. Band members get half-price drinks.

A new band with a home is a band that can build a base quickly. A new crackerjack band can also help the club increase its revenues and reputation. Early on, you may have to play for next to nothing but if you can draw, especially on a week night, it is a great place to prepare for bigger and better things. When you enter the wider world of bookings, you can take some of your homeboy fans with you.

THE CASUAL BOOKING AGREEMENT

It is a good reflection on a band to have a simple performance contract. Not only does it demonstrate that the band regards what they do as a business, it offers some degree of protection should things go sour on a gig. The one-page booking agreement that follows should suffice. A word of advice for private bookings: I recommend getting 50 percent of the performance fee as a non-refundable deposit and the balance of the performance fee to be paid in currency as soon as the sound check is completed. If a client hedges, just tell them that the band is a company and that the payment conditions are company policy. There is an old adage that possession is nine-tenths of the law and if the cash is in your hand at the time of performance you will have no worries about insufficient checks or a mother of the bride who doesn't like the mix and feels she deserves a deep discount. If a client wants to cancel a gig well before the date and it is likely that you will be able to replace it, you may consider refunding some or all of the deposit.

When dealing with a new venue, simple is better. Here's an example of a one-page booking agreement that will work nicely for a casual club booking. You will see it is a simple document that only covers when, where, and how much. There are no clauses about security (what happens if the band has a two-night stand and all their equipment is stolen from the stage after night one?) or other possible club liabilities. A contract that will take longer than one minute to read is not what a casual event buyer will be looking for. Many are not looking for a one-page agreement at all. They only want a handshake.

CASUAL BAND BOOKING AGREEMENT

THIS CONTRACT, entered into on this __ day of _____, 20__, is for the personal services of the Musician(s) for the performance described below. The undersigned Employer and the undersigned Musician(s) agree and contract as follows:

1.   **NAME OF MUSICIAN(S):**

2.   **NUMBER OF MUSICIAN(S):**

3.   **NAME AND ADDRESS OF PLACE OF PERFORMANCE**

4.   **DATE(S) OF PERFORMANCE:**

5.   **TIME(S) OF PERFORMANCE:**

6.   **WAGE AGREED UPON:**

7.   **DEPOSIT:**

8.   **PAYMENT OF BALANCE TO _____ MADE IN U.S. CURRENCY OR CERTIFIED CHECK AT THE END OF PERFORMANCE.**

9.   **ADDITIONAL TERMS:**

10.   This contract constitutes a complete and binding agreement between the Employer and the Musician(s). Agent acts only as agent and assumes no responsibility as between the Employer and the Musician(s).

11.   In case of breach of this contract by Employer, the Employer agrees to pay the amount stated in Section 6 as mitigated damages, plus reasonable attorney's fees, court costs, and legal interest.

13.   The Employer agrees to be responsible for harm, loss, or damage of any kind to musician(s) person or property while located at the place of performance (Section 3 herein).

14.   The persons signing for Employer and the Musician(s) agree to be personally, jointly and severally liable for the terms of this contract.

_____   _____
For Musicians   For Employer

As you can see, this describes the gig briefly and lets everyone know what is expected of them. More comprehensive booking and festival agreements covering such aspects as parking, security, merchandising, and other show modules may be found on the CD-ROM. If you sign with an agency or management firm, you will be using their booking contract form.

Taking Stock of Assets

One of my favorite ploys for a new band is to ask them what they feel their assets are. They will hem and haw for a few minutes and then come up with a number. That number in most cases, is low and there is another way of looking at it. The band comes into the meeting with a perception that they are broke. I beg to differ. When I asked the band to fill in an inventory sheet for me, by the time we added up all the assets, not held by the band per se, but by the component members, there was a value of almost $50,000 already in the equipment and vehicle equity. They went from broke to a bottom line of $50,000 in assets in less than an hour. Not that these assets are going to be pledged to the band as a common property, but it helps the starting band to realize they aren't complete paupers and have a bit of an equipment war chest. The Band Asset Inventory form (see page 54) is also on the CD-ROM with all the formulas in place in Excel format.

At each point along the way, the band is setting themselves up to be a player—not just on stage, but in the business arena. When a manager or record label comes along and sees the band has made this much effort in taking the business seriously, it inspires confidence in the band—not just as artists, but also as business associates. It causes other industry pros to think, "This act has their act together."

MUSIC BUSINESS CONTRACTS
BAND ASSET INVENTORY
* figures from Personal Inventory Worksheet

Total Band Assets	Fair Market Value	NOTES
Sound Equipment		
Musical Instruments		
Vehicles		
Computer Equipment		
Office Equipment		
Other Equipment		
Misc.		
Band Total		

MEMBER ONE	Fair Market Value
Sound Equipment	
Musical Instruments	
Vehicles	
Computer Equipment	
Office Equipment	
Other Equipment	
Misc.	
Total Member One	

MEMBER FOUR	Fair Market Value
Sound Equipment	
Musical Instruments	
Vehicles	
Computer Equipment	
Office Equipment	
Other Equipment	
Misc.	
Total Member Four	

MEMBER TWO	Fair Market Value
Sound Equipment	
Musical Instruments	
Vehicles	
Computer Equipment	
Office Equipment	
Other Equipment	
Misc.	
Total Member Two	

MEMBER FIVE	Fair Market Value
Sound Equipment	
Musical Instruments	
Vehicles	
Computer Equipment	
Office Equipment	
Other Equipment	
Misc.	
Total Member Five	

MEMBER THREE	Fair Market Value
Sound Equipment	
Musical Instruments	
Vehicles	
Computer Equipment	
Office Equipment	
Other Equipment	
Misc.	
Total Member Three	

MEMBER SIX	Fair Market Value
Sound Equipment	
Musical Instruments	
Vehicles	
Computer Equipment	
Office Equipment	
Other Equipment	
Misc.	
Total Member Six	

Part III

The Professionals

CHAPTER 6

Working with Agents

Claude Butch Morgan, Courtesy of The Music Office

I f an agent likes you, they may try to entice you into an exclusive arrangement. This can be a match made in heaven for the parties. A manager can off load the tour scheduling to the agent and let the agent bring him the tour dates as a complete package. If the agent is working the band in venues with good exposure, it will only help grow the fan base. On the other hand many bands have been worn down on the road to nowhere by playing venues and clubs that don't respond to that particular genre of music or band. A good agent knows both the venue and the act intimately and trusts that both parties will deliver the goods. A band's career can go down the drain "touring" little towns playing motel lounges and dancehalls demanding cover music. A few years of this can make a day job look positively cool.

A good booking agent can be a major asset to a performing artist's career. A good agent is always looking for new talent to add to the stable. It seems there are as many kinds of booking agents as there are musical genres. Many of the smaller agencies will focus on one musical or entertainment genre while the larger corporate agencies such as William Morris can represent a wide range of clientele from actors and musicians to authors and sports stars. The agent's job is to get as much work as possible at the best (largest) possible price. The agent is generally looking for three things in a new act: talent, reliability, and the prompt payment of their commissions. Regardless of how hot your band is, an agent will not book you for long if you are late to gigs, late on paying them, or act in other unprofessional manners.

When does an agent enter the picture? A good agent has a long list of contacts with venues, concert promoters, corporate buyers, and such. It is hard for a new agency to get off the ground as this network can take years to build. A new agent might be going to clubs to find that many already have an exclusive deal with a particular entertainment agency and aren't looking for new sources of talent.

Under the assumption that you got lucky and your agent is actually working to expand your career, let's take a look at how an exclusive agency arrangement develops.

THE EXCLUSIVE AGENT AGREEMENT

Agents sometimes work with bands on an exclusive basis as well as venues. A new band might want to approach a new agent with a "try before you buy" approach. The agent and band can enter into a 90-day exclusive agreement and see how it works out. The band would continue to play and book any venues where they have an existing relationship, but they would pay commissions on new gigs brought to the table. If the band doesn't get any more bookings with an agent than they were getting without one, after ninety days, they would be best to just walk away. If the agent found that the venues didn't like the act for whatever reason or the band was paying late on commissions, the agent can also walk away. The less acrimonious the split is the better. It is never a good thing to burn any bridges you don't have to in this business. Just because a business relationship didn't work out now doesn't mean it won't at some time in the future.

The agent's goal, if the band is promising, is to replace the existing gigs that the band may have brought to the table with better ones. The better the agent performs, the more likely the band can be enticed into a longer exclusive arrangement. Exclusivity isn't a necessity but if an agent hears that you are additionally using a competitor, it takes your band down the roster a peg or two. Agents will send the best work to their best bands and the ones that stay close to home.

EXCLUSIVE AGENT – MUSICIAN AGREEMENT

THIS AGREEMENT is for the services of music and/or entertainment described below between the undersigned Musician(s) (includes accompanying musicians and/or entertainers as described below, hereinafter referred to as "MUSICIAN") and the Agent who is to provide booking and management services (hereinafter referred to as "AGENT").

I. TERM OF AGREEMENT

This AGREEMENT begins on the _____ day of _____, 20_____, and the term shall be valid through the ____ day of _____, 20__, and shall be considered renewed at the end of the period herein unless Musician receives a written notice with the intent to terminate this contract. Any questions relating to this agreement shall be interpreted in accordance with the laws of the State of _____.

II. SCOPE OF AGREEMENT

MUSICIAN(s) hereby employs AGENT and AGENT hereby accepts employment as MUSICIAN'S exclusive booking agent, manager and representative throughout the world for services, appearances and endeavors. "A.F.M." as used herein refers to the American Federation of Musicians of the United States of America and Canada.

III. DUTIES OF AGENT

a) AGENT agrees to use reasonable efforts performing the following duties: assist MUSICIAN in obtaining and negotiating engagements for the MUSICIAN'S professional career; promote and publicize MUSICIAN'S name and talents; business correspondence on MUSICIAN'S behalf; cooperate with duly constituted and authorized representatives of MUSICIAN in the performance of such duties.

b) AGENT will maintain office, staff and facilities reasonably adequate to perform these services. MUSICIAN is familiar with AGENT'S present office, staff and facilities and acknowledges these as reasonably adequate.

c) AGENT shall maintain such records as may be required by the State of _____ pursuant to any laws governing this industry or agreement.

Page 1 of 4

IV. RIGHTS OF AGENT

a) AGENT may render similar services to others and may engage in other business and ventures.

b) MUSICIAN will promptly refer to AGENT all communications, written or oral, received by or on behalf of MUSICIAN.

c) MUSICIAN will not engage any other person, firm or corporation to perform AGENT'S services (except a personal manager) or perform or appear professionally or offer to do so, except through AGENT.

d) AGENT may publicize the fact that he or she is the exclusive booking agent and representative for MUSICIAN.

e) AGENT shall have the right to use or to permit others to use MUSICIAN'S name and likeness for advertising or publicity relating to MUSICIAN'S services and appearances (without cost or expense to MUSICIAN, unless MUSICIAN agrees in writing).

f) In the event of MUSICIAN'S breach of this AGREEMENT, AGENT'S sole right and remedy shall be the receipt of the commissions specified in this AGREEMENT from MUSICIAN, but only if MUSICIAN receives money or other consideration on which commissions are payable [except as provided in paragraph 5 (c)].

V. COMPENSATION OF AGENT

a) MUSICIAN agrees to pay the following commissions on the gross funds directly or indirectly received by MUSICIAN for each engagement:

   i) **Twenty (20%) percent** of the gross funds received for a single night or two consecutive night engagement at the same place.

   ii) **Fifteen (15%) percent** of all gross funds received for three or more consecutive night engagements at the same place.

b) Commissions shall be due and payable to AGENT by check or money order. Funds must be payable to _____ for the full amount due within seventy-two (72) hours after completion of engagement. In the event MUSICIAN fails to pay any commissions when due, AGENT may, at his or her discretion, refuse to secure further engagements for MUSICIAN until said commissions are paid. The refusal to secure further engagements for MUSICIAN because of failure to pay shall not constitute a breach on the part of AGENT to secure the minimum number of engagements provided hereunder. The minimum number of engagements guaranteed pursuant to paragraph 6(b) shall be reduced by either:

   I) One (1) week for six night engagements, or

   ii) Two (2) engagements for single night engagements for each week the commission remains due and payable.

c) No commissions shall be payable on any engagement if MUSICIAN is not paid for such engagement, and only if non-payment is not due to MUSICIAN'S misconduct. If non-payment for all or part of engagement is the fault of MUSICIAN, the full commission for the contract price will be paid to AGENT. This shall not preclude AGENT from seeking and recovering damages to compensate for actual expenses incurred as the direct result of the cancellation of an engagement when such cancellation was the result of the intentional misconduct of the MUSICIAN.

d) As used in this paragraph and elsewhere in this AGREEMENT, the term "gross earnings" shall mean the gross funds received by MUSICIAN for each engagement.

VI. DURATION AND TERMINATION OF AGREEMENT

a) The term of this AGREEMENT shall be as stated in the opening heading, subject to termination by either party upon the default of the other of any provision in this AGREEMENT.

b) In addition to termination pursuant to other provisions of this AGREEMENT, this AGREEMENT may be terminated by either party, by notice as provided below, if MUSICIAN:

   i) does not obtain employment for at least _____ cumulative weeks of up to six night engagements to be performed during each year during the term hereof; or

   ii) does not obtain employment for at least _____ single night engagements to be performed during each year of the term hereof.

c) Notice of such termination because of default of either party shall be given by mail addressed to the addressee at his last known address. At such time the MUSICIAN will play out those engagements specified and contracted by AGENT.

d) This contract remains in effect even if the MUSICIAN joins or becomes a member of A.F.M. or other musician union.

VII. NO OTHER AGREEMENTS

This is the only AGREEMENT between the parties involved. There is no other agreement, arrangement, or participation between the parties which are not created by this AGREEMENT.

VIII. SUBMISSION AND DETERMINATION OF DISPUTES

GOVERNING LAW: This AGREEMENT shall be governed by the laws and in the courts of the State of _____ and by the laws of the United States, excluding their conflicts of law principles. Any dispute or legal proceeding regarding the AGREEMENT shall take place in the county of _____, in the State of _____.

IX. NO ASSIGNMENT OF THIS AGREEMENT

This AGREEMENT shall be personal to the parties and not transferable without the prior written consent of the MUSICIAN and AGENT. The obligations imposed by this AGREEMENT shall be binding. MUSICIAN may terminate this AGREEMENT in writing at any time within ninety (90) days from the date of this AGREEMENT.

X. DAMAGES

In view of the fact that MUSICIAN is able to secure employment at establishments throughout the United States and the world and is further able to secure agents throughout the same area, it is difficult and costly for AGENT to ascertain the names of agents subsequently engaged by MUSICIAN or to ascertain the number of or value of subsequent engagements undertaken by MUSICIAN. The parties agree that in the event of MUSICIAN'S breach of this AGREEMENT either by securing bookings from another agent or person or by refusing bookings secured by AGENT, then AGENT'S damages shall be determined as follows:

a) For each remaining month of this AGREEMENT after MUSICIAN'S breach, AGENT shall be entitled to receive as damages an amount equal to the average monthly commissions to which AGENT was entitled prior to MUSICIAN'S breach. The average commission shall be based on actual engagements by MUSICIAN as well as bookings refused by MUSICIAN.

b) AGENT shall be further entitled to receive his or her costs, disbursements and attorney's fees as provided by law in any suit to collect damages provided herein.

XI. A.F.M. MEMBERSHIP

By executing this AGREEMENT, MUSICIAN does not obligate himself in any way to become a member of the A.F.M., notwithstanding any agreement AGENT may have with A.F.M.

XII. TERMS

All terms expressed in the singular shall also mean the plural and all terms implying gender shall mean either gender.

DATED: _____

For AGENT

_____
Signature

_____
Name

_____
Address

_____
City/State/Zip

_____
Telephone

For MUSICIAN

_____
Signature

_____
Name

_____
Address

_____
City/State/Zip

_____
Telephone

Let's take a brief look at the main components of this exclusive agency agreement. There are some points that may warrant drilling down a bit.

The preamble is self explanatory so let's jump down the page a bit to Section IV and pick it apart.

IV. RIGHTS OF AGENT
a) AGENT may render similar services to others and may engage in other business and ventures.

Agents almost always represent more than one artist and this is an industry standard. Asking an agent to book you exclusively is wasted breath.

b) MUSICIAN will promptly refer to AGENT all communications, written or oral, received by or on behalf of MUSICIAN.

The agent will need the space to do the job and this is an important clause as artists that have been booking themselves are reluctant to shell out a percentage of a gig when the venue approaches the artist. I have seen a number of artist-agent relationships go down the tube when the artist tries to "moonlight" behind the agent's back. When signed exclusively to an agent, let the agent do their job and refer all inquiries to them.

a) MUSICIAN will not engage any other person, firm or corporation to perform AGENT'S services (except a personal manager) or perform or appear professionally or offer to do so, except through AGENT.

This underlines clause (b) and gives you an idea of how important agents see this.

b) AGENT may publicize the fact that he or she is the exclusive booking agent and representative for MUSICIAN.

The agent will make the call on what promotional material to use. It is a good idea to feed the agent only the "greatest hits" of the band's promotional arsenal. It is likely that if you have progressed to the point where an agent is willing to take a shot on you, your promo probably already looks pretty good.

c) AGENT shall have the right to use or to permit others to use MUSICIAN'S name and likeness for advertising or publicity relating to MUSICIAN'S services and appearances (without cost or expense to MUSICIAN, unless MUSICIAN agrees in writing).

This is specifying that the promotional materials will be produced and paid for by the agent. The agent will certainly brand your photos, biography, and repertoire with their logo, name, address, and phone number.

d) In the event of MUSICIAN'S breach of this AGREEMENT, Agent's sole right and remedy shall be the receipt of the commissions specified in this AGREEMENT from MUSICIAN, but only if MUSICIAN receives money or other consideration on which commissions are payable [except as provided in paragraph 5(c)].

This is a clause that many agents might delete or modify as it limits their recourse should the band violate the terms of the exclusive agreement or one of the individual concert contracts.

If I was approaching this from the band side I would want this clause or something like it in the contract. If I was the agent, I would delete this clause and leave the door open to greater remedies in case of default.

Section V. of the exclusive agent agreement specifies the agent's commission rate. It also specifies when and how the agent expects to be paid. Section V makes interesting reading:

No commissions shall be payable on any engagement if MUSICIAN is not paid for such engagement, and only if non-payment is not due to MUSICIAN'S misconduct. If non-payment for all or part of engagement is the fault of MUSICIAN, the full commission for the contract price will be paid to Agent. This shall not preclude Agent from seeking and recovering damages to compensate for actual expenses incurred as the direct result of the cancellation of an engagement when such cancellation was the result of the intentional misconduct of the MUSICIAN.

If you screw up at the venue and the venue decides to send you packing without pay, you still owe the agent the commission. This is an agent's worse nightmare. A group they send out gets caught in the parking lot with dope and underage girls and gets the boot. The agent may very well lose the account because of the incident and if the venue is a regular client, this incident could cost the agent a great deal of money. As an example, the Wand Dang Club fires a band without pay for misconduct of whatever nature and the club decides to sever the relationship with the agent. The agent might look at it as an account that has been serviced for years and was bringing the agency $1,500 a month in commissions. Those commissions are now gone and the band is to blame for the agent's loss of $18,000 a year because of the band's actions. Speaking of actions, this is what an agent might consider actionable as in suing you for damages and lost commissions.

In Section VI we have an issue to address:

VI. DURATION AND TERMINATION OF AGREEMENT
a) The term of this AGREEMENT shall be as stated in the opening heading, subject to termination by either party upon the default of the other of any provision in this AGREEMENT.

At the beginning of the contract, the term of the agreement is specified but there is a problem. Let's read the opening paragraph:

THIS AGREEMENT begins on the _____ day of _____, 20_____, and the term shall be valid through the ___ day of _____, 20__, and shall be considered renewed at the end of the period herein unless MUSICIAN receives a written notice with the intent to terminate this contract. Any questions relating to this agreement shall be interpreted in accordance with the laws of the State of _____.

The first thing that jumps out at me (coming from the band's point of view) is that the contract remains binding for the artist but not the agent. This could be amended to include a band option to notify the agent in writing at the end of the term that they are severing the relationship.

There are other clauses for the termination of the agreement based on the agent's performance. These clauses can be easily tweaked to reflect the reality of the situation. For example, it is very unlikely that a band performing original music will be getting one-week stands while on the road. The rest of the performance benchmarks should remain. Keep in mind that the agent's job is to increase your performance revenues. Filling in these blanks sets the performance benchmark so make sure that it is a good distance from where you already are.

a) In addition to termination pursuant to other provisions of this AGREEMENT, this AGREEMENT may be terminated by either party, by notice as provided below, if MUSICIAN:

i) does not obtain employment for at least _____ cumulative weeks of up to six night engagements to be performed during each year during the term hereof; or

ii) does not obtain employment for at least _____ single night engagements to be performed during each year of the term hereof.

b) Notice of such termination because of default of either party shall be given by mail addressed to the addressee at his last known address. At such time the MUSICIAN will play out those engagements specified and contracted by AGENT.

This could be modified to remind the agent that the continuation of the relationship during the initial term of the agreement is an "at will" arrangement for both parties.

Should things go sour between the parties, we have Section X. standing by to show the penalties for violation of the agreement by the artist.

X. DAMAGES
In view of the fact that MUSICIAN is able to secure employment at establishments throughout the United States and the world and is further able to secure agents throughout the same area, it is difficult and costly for AGENT to ascertain the names of agents subsequently engaged by MUSICIAN or to ascertain the number

of or value of subsequent engagements undertaken by MUSICIAN. The parties agree that in the event of MUSICIAN'S breach of this AGREEMENT either by securing bookings from another agent or person or by refusing bookings secured by AGENT, then AGENT'S damages shall be determined as follows:

a) For each remaining month of this AGREEMENT after MUSICIAN'S breach, AGENT shall be entitled to receive as damages an amount equal to the average monthly commissions to which AGENT was entitled prior to MUSICIAN'S breach. The average commission shall be based on actual engagements by MUSICIAN as well as bookings refused by MUSICIAN.

b) AGENT shall be further entitled to receive his or her costs, disbursements and attorney's fees as provided by law in any suit to collect damages provided herein.

As mentioned above, an agent can suffer loss of revenues and reputation when an artist on the roster causes trouble or violates the agreement. These terms are entirely fair for both the musician and the agent. The musician at this time has broken the promise not to approach other agents during the term of the contract. The agent is due compensation for this violation. This is not always a bad thing for a band or a talent-stealing agent though. Should the band acquire next level management or a label deal that has catapulted them into the public eye and the next level of personal appearances, a new agent viewing the band with greed might think it a bargain to pay off the old agent the balance of the estimated commissions earned and make a clean break. If the old agent was booking the group for $800 a night and the new agent has them on a national tour pulling $5,000 nightly, it would only take the new agent a few performances to recoup in commissions what it cost to buy off the old agent. If time goes by and the band falls from national grace, they may still have a friend with the original agent on the way down because they left under, if not ethically, at least legally sound circumstances where the agent got some compensation.

You will notice that the signature line at the end of the contract is for the agent and musician. Some agents require the signatures of all the individual band members; thus, making them equally liable. So, if you have done your homework from previous chapters, the agent will realize that the new client isn't a group of individuals at all, but a bona fide business with a real name, checking account, and tax ID number. It will be much more impressive than a band that asks the agent to cash the check because none of the band members have bank accounts.

CHAPTER 7

Working with Publishers

Tom Paxton, Courtesy of The Music Office

A bit further down the road of a writer's career the music publisher may enter the story. A publisher's job is to take the song or catalog and derive as much income as possible from it. The publisher may have connections to sales outlets such as film sound tracks, foreign licensing, and other avenues that a songwriter may not have access to. Most successful songwriters are signed to a major publisher and enjoy a long relationship with them.

Let's take a moment to discuss the rather arcane way songwriter/composer royalties are looked at. There are actually two components to the publishing side of a song: the writer side and the publisher side. These two pieces of the pie are equal in size (see the left chart on the following page).

A Song Divided

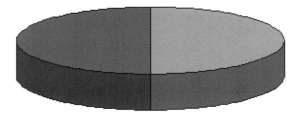
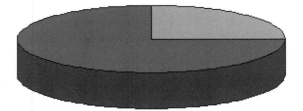

■ Publisher Portion

■ Writer Portion

In the chart on the right side (above), we have one song split into two unequal components. The writer's share is much less than the publisher's share. In the case of a known and proven songwriter, the writer might have enough leverage to change the equation a bit. Although the writer's share in publishing is protected by law, the publisher's portion is negotiable. A writer with hit songs under their belt could hold all the writer royalties and half the publishing as seen in the second chart.

The contractual terms of an agreement between a songwriter and a publisher again depends on the negotiating strength of each position. A major publisher with thousands of songs in their catalog, many of them hits, can open many doors for an emerging writer. A startup publisher with only your songs in their catalog may harvest different results. Any relationship with a startup publisher should be with a reversion clause based on performance. A writer can be willing to give a new publisher a shot, but only if it pays off and soon. On the other hand, when you are giving a publisher the exclusive rights to pitch the song, whether they paid for it or not, give them ample time to shop it around. A six-month to one-year period should be sufficient for your publisher to exhaust his leads.

The best way to approach a publisher is with a single song deal with options for renewal and/or reversion between both parties. If the publisher can't place a song in a given period, the rights revert to the writer. If the publisher delivers, the writer agrees to assign the rights to the publisher. If both parties are satisfied, they can move on to a broader relationship involving more compositions or even an exclusive writing agreement.

It is not always necessary to have a publisher, even if you have found some success. Writers in certain niche markets such as Tejano, rap, and other genres can successfully publish their own songs and leave the administration to a third-party publisher. Many artists who own their own catalogs allow Bug Music to administer the songs. Bug is a worldwide company and can enforce the publishing copyrights in markets and countries the writer has never heard of. Bug Music makes sure that the accounting and enforcement components are in place and takes care of all the paperwork. Again, the rate or percentage of the money shared with Bug Music depends on the strength of the writer and catalog, typically between 6-30 percent. If I was a band that was licensing recordings to a European label for example, I might look at Bug to administer my publishing rights in that market.

Let's take a look at the three most common publishing deals: the option, the single song agreement, and the exclusive songwriter agreement. We'll start with the option which is tied to a more comprehensive second agreement should the song find placement.

SINGLE SONG OPTION

As you can see, the simple one-page contract rider (shown on page 72) protects both the writer and publisher during a trial period. Essentially, the writer owes the publisher nothing during this trial period except the right to exclusively market the song. The publisher is protected by this exclusivity and it will continue for the life of the copyright should the publisher place the song. The publisher is responsible only for promoting and placing the song, not defending it legally against any litigation that may arise due to copyright infringement or other cause. Think of it as your prenuptial agreement with what might be a life-long partner.

SINGLE SONG OPTION

ADDENDUM TO AGREEMENT DATED: _____ day of _____, 20_____.

SINGLE SONG OPTION:

The WRITER and PUBLISHER do hereby agree to the terms of the aforementioned Agreement under the following terms and conditions:

1.PUBLISHER agrees that if the song now entitled
_____
is not assigned a mechanical license to be recorded and released to the general public on phonorecords by the _____ day of _____, 20____, the PUBLISHER shall relinquish and return all rights and copyrights to the WRITER.

2.The WRITER shall not be held responsible for any payment to the PUBLISHER regardless of the amount PUBLISHER may have spent on the recording, development, promotion, or any other expense incurred by PUBLISHER relating to this song.

3.In the event PUBLISHER is responsible for the placement of said musical composition on phonorecords released to the public, WRITER hereby agrees to honor and uphold the Publishing Agreement to which this is an Addendum.

4.WRITER agrees that the Publishing Agreement shall be in force and binding during this option period and will not assign the rights to the aforementioned song to any other until this Addendum has expired.

5.During this option period, PUBLISHER shall not be required to defend WRITER against any legal action against WRITER for copyright infringement, or any other proprietary right. After this option period has expired with the song recorded on phonorecord, and the Publishing Agreement to which this is an Addendum is in effect, PUBLISHER will defend the WRITER under the terms outlined in Article II of the Publishing Agreement.

6.GOVERNING LAW: This Agreement shall be governed by the laws and in the courts of the State of _____ and by the laws of the United States, excluding their conflicts of law principles. Any dispute or legal proceeding regarding the Agreement shall take place in the county of _____, in the State of _____.

We, the undersigned, do hereby acknowledge and agree to the terms of this agreement.

DATED: _____

AGREED TO AND ACCEPTED

_____   _____
For PUBLISHER   For WRITER

If things work out and the song is placed by the publisher, the second contract, the industry standard song assignment of rights kicks in. This is where the song becomes the property of the publisher in exchange for exploiting the song commercially, administering the accounting, and defending the copyright against all infringers. This contract is much more comprehensive and is most often tied to the length of the copyright which will span many decades.

SONG PUBLISHING AGREEMENT

PUBLISHING AGREEMENT

AGREEMENT made this ___ day of _____, 20__ between _____ (hereinafter designated as "Publisher") and _____ (hereinafter individually, jointly, and/or (severally designated as "Writer(s)").

       In consideration of the Agreement herein contained and for the sum of ONE DOLLAR and other good and valuable considerations in hand paid by Publisher to the Writer(s), receipt of which is hereby acknowledged, the parties agree as follows:

1.   The Writer(s) hereby sells, assigns, transfers and delivers to the Publisher, its successors and assigns, a certain heretofore unpublished original musical composition, written and/or composed by the above named Writer(s), now entitled:

including the title, words, and music, and all copyrights thereof, including but not limited to the copyright registration thereof No._____, and all rights, claims and demands in any way relating thereto, and the Exclusive right to secure copyright therein throughout the world, and to have and to hold the said copyrights and all rights of whatsoever nature now and hereafter for and during the full terms of all of said copyrights. In consideration of the agreement to pay royalties herein contained and other good and valuable consideration in hand paid by Publisher to the Writer(s), receipt of which is hereby acknowledged, the Writer(s) hereby sells, assigns, transfers and delivers to the Publisher, its successors and assigns, all renewals and extensions of the copyrights of said composition to which the Writer(s) may be entitled hereafter and all registrations thereof, and all rights of any and all nature now and hereafter hereunder existing, for the full terms of all renewals and extensions of copyrights.

2.   The Writer(s) hereby warrant and represent that said composition is his/her (their) sole, exclusive and original work, of which the title, music and lyric was written and composed by him/her (them), that said composition is new and original and does not infringe any other copyrighted works, that he/she (they) has the full right and power to enter into this Agreement, that said composition has not heretofore been published, that said composition is innocent and does not contain any matter which, if published or otherwise used, will be proprietary right at common law or any statutory copyright or penal law, and that he/she (they) will hold harmless and defend the Publisher against any suit, claim, demand, or recovery by reason of any violation of any of the representations, warranties of covenants right or copyright or any injurious matter in the said composition, actual or claimed and the Publisher is hereby granted the right, in event of any such claim or claims, to make such defense as may be advised by counsel and the costs and counsel fees therefore together with any damages sustained and amounts of any such settlements shall be charged to and paid for by the Writer(s).

3.   In consideration of this Agreement, the Publisher agrees to pay the Writer(s) jointly, during the original and renewal terms of the copyright throughout the world as follows:

      (a)   In respect of regular piano copies sold and paid for at wholesale in the United States and Canada, royalties of **FIVE (5) CENTS** per copy.

      (b)   A royalty of **FIVE (5) CENTS** per copy of dance orchestrations sold and paid for in the United States and Canada.

Page 1 of 4

(c)   A royalty of **FIFTY (50%) PERCENT** of all net earned sums received by the Publisher in respect to regular piano copies and/or orchestrations sold and paid for in any foreign country by a foreign publisher.

(d)   The sum of **ONE DOLLAR** as and when the composition is published in any folio or composite work or lyric magazine by the Publisher or licensees of the Publisher. Such publications may be made at the discretion of the Publisher.

(e)   As to "professional material" not sold or resold, no royalty shall be payable.

(f)   An amount equal to FIFTY (50%) percent of all net earned proceeds received and retained by the Publisher arising out of:

     (i)   the manufacture and sale of phonograph records and other parts of instruments serving to mechanically reproduce the composition

     (ii)   the synchronization of the composition with motion pictures, and

     (iii)   the recording of the composition on electrical transcriptions; provided however that if the Publisher administers the licenses for the aforementioned uses through an agent, trustee of another administrator who is not in the exclusive employ of the Publisher (i.e. Harry Fox as Trustee), the Publisher, in determining its receipts shall be entitled to deduct from gross license fees paid by the licensees a sum equal to the charges paid by the Publisher to said agent, trustee, or administrate, and said deduction in no event is to exceed Ten (10%) percent of the license fees.

(g)   Except as herein expressly provided, no other royalties shall be paid in respect of the composition.

4.   The Publisher agrees to render to the Writer(s), jointly, on or about February 15th and August 15th of each year, during which income is received by the Publisher in respect of said musical composition, covering the six months ending December 31st and June 30th of each such year respectively, royalty statements accompanied by remittances for all sums shown to be due thereunder. Any such statements shall be binding upon the Writer(s) after it has been rendered to the Writer(s) unless Writer(s) have objected to it in writing during the period of One (1) year after the date of each royalty statement by registered mail return receipt requested.

5.   It is understood and agreed by and between all of the parties hereto that all royalties payable hereunder to the writer(s) jointly shall be divided and paid among them respectively as follows:

NAME	SHARE	% PERCENT
_____	_____	_____
_____	_____	_____
_____	_____	_____

6.   Anything to the contrary notwithstanding, nothing in this Agreement contained shall obligate the Publisher to print copies of said composition or shall prevent the Publisher from

authorizing publishers, agents, and representatives in countries inside and outside of the United States from exercising exclusive publication and all other rights in foreign countries in compensation of the customary royalty basis, it being understood that the percentage of the Writer's royalty on monies received from foreign sources shall be computed on the Publisher's net receipts; and nothing in this Agreement shall prevent the Publisher from authorizing publishers in the United States from exercising exclusive publication rights and other rights in the United States in said composition, provided the Publisher shall pay Writer(s) the royalties herein stipulated.

7.   The Writer(s) hereby consent to such changes, adaptations, dramatizations, editing and arrangements of said composition, and the setting of words to the music and of music to the words, and the change of title as Publisher deems desirable. The Writer(s) hereby waive and all claims which they have or may have against the Publisher and/or its associated, affiliated and subsidiary corporations by reason of the fact that the title of said composition may be the same or similar to that of any musical composition or compositions hereto or hereafter acquired by the Publisher and/or its associated, affiliated and subsidiary corporations.

8.   The Writer(s) individually and jointly consent to the use of their respective names, likenesses and biographical material and the title of said musical composition in connection with the titles and contents of folios of Musical compositions containing said composition with other musical compositions and in connection with publicity and advertising concerning the Publisher, its successors, assigns or licensees. Writer(s) agree that the use of said names, likenesses, biographical material and the title may commence prior to publication and may continue so long as the Publisher shall own and/or exercise rights in said composition.

9.   Written demands and notices other than royalty statements provided herein shall be sent by registered mail.

10.   Any legal action brought by Publisher against any alleged infringer of said composition shall be initiated and prosecuted at the Publisher's sole expense, and of any recovery made by it as a result thereof, after deduction for the expense of litigation, a sum equal to Fifty (50%) shall be paid to the Writer(s).

  (a)   If a claim is presented against the Publisher in respect of said composition, and because thereof the Publisher is jeopardized, it shall thereupon serve written notice upon the Writer(s), containing the full details of such claim known to the Publisher and thereafter until the claim has been adjudicated or settled shall hold any monies coming due the Writer(s) in escrow pending the outcome of such claim or claims. The Publisher shall have the right to settle or otherwise dispose of such claims in any manner as it, in its sole discretion, may determine. In the event of any recovery against the Publi`sher, either by way of judgement or settlement, all of the costs, charges, imbursements, attorney fees and the amount of the judgement or settlement may be deducted by the Publisher from any and all royalties or other payments therefore and thereafter payable to the Writer(s) by the Publisher or by its associated, affiliated or subsidiary corporation.

  (b)   From and after the service of summons in a suit for infringement filed against the Publisher with respect to said composition any and all payments thereafter coming due the Writer(s) shall be held by the Publisher in trust until the suit has been adjudicated or settled, then be disbursed accordingly, unless Writer(s) shall elect to file an acceptable bond in the sum of payments in which event sums due shall be paid Writer(s).

11.   "Writer(s)" as used herein shall be deemed to include all authors and composers signing this agreement.

12.   The Writer(s) each for him or herself, hereby irrevocably constitute and appoint the Publisher or any of its officers, directors, or general manager, his (their) attorney and representative, in the names(s) of the Writer(s), or any of them, or in the name of the Publisher, his successors and assigns, to make, sign, execute, acknowledge and deliver any and all instruments which may be desirable or necessary in order to vest in the Publisher, its successors and assigns, any of the rights herein referred to.

13.   The Publisher shall have the right to sell, assign, transfer, license or otherwise dispose of any and all its rights in whole or part under this Agreement to any person, firm, or corporation, but said disposition shall not affect the right of Writer(s) to the royalties herein set forth.

14.   This agreement shall be construed only under the laws of the State of _____. If any part of this agreement shall be held invalid or unenforceable, it shall not affect the validity of the balance of this Agreement.

15.   This Agreement shall be binding upon and shall inure to the benefit of the respective parties hereto, their respective successor's interest, legal representatives and assigns, and represents the entire understanding between the parties.

IN WITNESS WHEREOF, the parties have hereunder set their names the day and year first above written.

Date:_____

BY:_____   By:_____
  WRITER   **PUBLISHER**

Song Publishing Agreement Summary

Let's look at a few of the more salient clauses in the Song Publishing Agreement contract. Don't be put off by the amount of "One Dollar" at the beginning of the contract. It is a common figure that is found in contracts where the payment from one party to the other is in the future and somewhat speculative. Specifying one dollar doesn't value the deal, it just specifies that something of specific value, albeit a low one, changed hands at signing. Make sure to frame your one dollar advance.

Paragraph 2: As a writer, you should pay close attention to Paragraph 2. In this paragraph you make the claim to be the author and that you are not infringing on any other copyright. It also makes the claim that no other publisher has been assigned rights. This brings to mind an old Nashville anecdote.

A handsome young singer-songwriter carrying a guitar enters the office of an old and jaded Nashville publisher.

"Mr. Publisher, I've got this great song you've got to hear. You're gonna love it."

"Okay kid, I'll bite. Show me what you've got."

The kid whips out his guitar and plays the song. It is a very good song; a potential hit. The kid has a good voice and is making a great delivery. The publisher is impressed.

"Well sonny, you're right there. It's a dandy of a song; still a little rough but shows a lot of promise."

"A little rough?" asks the songwriter.

"It just needs a bit of tweaking. You know add a word here take another away there. Just small time touch up but I'll tell you what. I'll go out on a limb and publish this song for you. I'll shape it up with some other words and we will co-write. Now don't get me wrong, your name will always appear first under the composer's name but I will get some credit too."

"That sounds okay to me but I didn't hear you talk about any money or recording or nothing like that."

"I can see you know your stuff and are going to strike a hard bargain so let's not beat around the bush. I will share co-authoring with you. I will publish the songs for you under the standard agreement. In addition, and I hope you are listening, I will record the song and pay you a royalty of 10 percent of the net profits from the sales of your recording. How's that for a great deal?"

The musician scratches his head for a moment, "Sounds like a pretty good deal to me but I still haven't heard about any money, as in soon."

"I'm trying to help you here son. I'm bringing years of experience and connections to the table but to show my fairness here's $100 as a show of good faith. That's all I have on me right now. Just sign here."

"Now you're talking! You got a deal."

After signing the deal the kid leaves and the publisher calls his friend.

"Murray you aren't gonna believe this. I just heard the best tune in a year and got the kid to sign over half the writer's stake and all the publishing. He also let me get away with the 10 percent of net profit royalty clause on a recording deal. There won't be much net profit after we promote the song over "recoupable" drinks at our 5-star hotel in Cannes, at MIDEM in France next January. All this for only $100! Poor idiot just lost a ton of money and walked out of here grinning ear to ear! There's a sucker born every minute."

Outside a car pulls up to the curb and the songwriter gets in. A friend is driving.

"Well did he try to screw you?"

The songwriter nods, "Yup he sure did. Told me about what a pal he was as he bent me over. I sold him half the song and all the publishing for $100."

The songwriter opens a shoebox on the seat and tosses in the hundred dollar bill to join many others. "That's the fifteenth publisher today that tried to screw us on the same song. There's a sucker born every minute."

The updated version of this song has the Harvard MBA publisher paying $10,000 for the rights to "Blue Eyes Crying in the Rain," a song he's never heard.

The bottom line is that if you are in violation of someone's copyright and they sue you, you have to join your publisher in the defense. After all, it is you who is being accused of violating the copyright. In the event that the entity doing the suing prevails, you are on your own as such a judgment would find you in violation of your agreement with the publisher.

Paragraph 7: This allows the publisher to modify the song in any way they see fit to exploit it. This is why you hear Beatle's songs with Ford Explorer lyrics. If Lennon/McCartney still had rights to the catalog instead of Michael Jackson, this probably wouldn't happen. When you sign the song away to a publisher you are giving them the go ahead to maximize earnings by whatever means. This used to be called "selling out" and is now part and parcel of the music business landscape.

Paragraph 10: This paragraph reflects what things will look like if your publisher winds up suing someone else for violating your copyright. The publisher will take on a much more aggressive stance as the infringement litigation might mean some monetary damages paid by the defendant upon the publisher and writer prevailing in court.

Paragraph 13: This makes the song and the publishing agreement assignable to other third parties. If the publishing company gets gobbled up by a corporate multi-national, the catalog and your song go with it. This is how Michael Jackson came to own the Beatles catalog; when Apple Music put the catalog on sale, Jackson outbid Paul McCartney.

There are other variations in publishing deals that have come onto the playing field in recent years. They go under names like "Song Royalty Sharing Agreement," and "Media Rights Agreements." You will find examples of these contracts on the CD-ROM accompanying this book. They are essentially the same as a single song agreement, but some of them bring more to the table such as a publisher's duty to promote the song in certain ways (i.e., cut demos) and performance kick-outs.

EXCLUSIVE SONGWRITER CONTRACT

Another common songwriter scenario is becoming a staff writer for a publisher. This can be as formal as actually showing up to an office and sitting down and writing tunes either alone or with a team of staff writers. Collaborative environments have brought us some of the greatest hits ever. Let's take a look at an exclusive deal between the songwriter and his publisher.

EXCLUSIVE SONGWRITER CONTRACT

THIS AGREEMENT is for the services of music and/or entertainment described below between the undersigned Artist(s) [includes accompanying musicians and/or entertainers as described below, hereinafter referred to as "WRITER(s)"] and the Publisher who is to provide services (hereinafter referred to as "PUBLISHER").

FOR AND IN CONSIDERATION OF mutual covenants set forth, the parties do hereby agree as follows:

Term: The term of this AGREEMENT shall commence today and continue until _____, 20____.

Employment: PUBLISHER employs WRITER to render services as a songwriter and composer. WRITER hereby accepts such employment and agrees to render such services exclusively for PUBLISHER during the length of this contract, upon the terms and conditions set forth.

Grant of Rights: WRITER grants to PUBLISHER the results and proceeds of WRITER's services, including, but not limited to the titles, words, and music of any and all original arrangements of musical compositions in the public domain. Attached as Exhibit A is a list of musical compositions written and made as part of this AGREEMENT.

WRITER acknowledges that included within the rights and interests is WRITER'S irrevocable grant to PUBLISHER, its successors, licensees, and sublicensees, of the sole and exclusive license, privilege, and authority of said original musical compositions and original arrangements in the public domain, whether now in existence or created during the term as follows:

(a) To perform said musical compositions publicly, whether for profit or otherwise, in public or private performance, radio broadcasting, television, or any and all means;

(b) To substitute a new title or titles, to make any arrangement, adaptation, translation, dramatization or transportation, and to add new lyrics to the music of any said compositions or new music, in whole or in part, as PUBLISHER may deem expedient or desirable. However, nothing contained herein shall allow PUBLISHER to make any changes in WRITER'S recorded performances. In the event PUBLISHER is directly involved in the printing of sheet music containing WRITER'S musical compositions, PUBLISHER agrees to make all reasonable effort to produce a reproduction of WRITER'S original recording of such composition as accurately as possible.

(c) To secure copyright registration and protection of said compositions in PUBLISHER'S name at his or her own cost, including any and all renewals and extensions of copyrights.

(d) To make or license others to make, master records, transcriptions, sound tracks, pressings, and any other mechanical, electrical or other productions of said compositions, in whole or part, in such form or manner and as frequently as PUBLISHER'S discretion shall determine. This includes the right to synchronize the same with sound motion pictures, and the right to manufacture, advertise, license or sell such reproductions for any and all purposes, including public and private performances, radio broadcasts, television, sound motion pictures, wired radio or cable television, phonograph records and any and all other means or devices.

(e) To print, publish and sell, and to license others to print, publish and sell, sheet music, orchestrations, arrangements and other editions of said compositions in all forms, including any or all of said compositions in song folios, song books, mixed or lyric magazines with or without music.

(f) Without any additional compensation, WRITER grants PUBLISHER the perpetual right to use and publish and to permit others to use and publish WRITER'S name (including any professional name adopted by WRITER), WRITER'S photograph or any other likeness (which shall be approved by WRITER), biographical material concerning WRITER, and the titles of any and all of the compositions in connection with the printing, sale, advertising, performance and distribution of the compositions. This right shall be exclusive during the term of this agreement and nonexclusive thereafter. WRITER grants PUBLISHER the right to refer to WRITER as PUBLISHER'S "Exclusive Songwriter and Composer" or any other similar appropriate designation, during the term of this contract.

Power of Attorney: WRITER hereby authorizes and appoints PUBLISHER, or any of its officers, WRITER'S true and lawful attorney (with full power of substitution and delegation), in WRITER'S name, and in WRITER'S place and stead, or in PUBLISHER'S name,

Compensation: Provided the WRITER shall faithfully and completely perform the terms, covenants and conditions of this AGREEMENT, PUBLISHER hereby agrees to provide the following compensation to WRITER for the services to be rendered under this AGREEMENT:

(a) Ten percent (10%) of the wholesale selling price per copy for each piano copy and dance orchestration printed, published and sold in the United States and Canada by PUBLISHER or its licensees, for which payment has been received by PUBLISHER, after deduction of returns.

(b) Twelve and one-half percent (12-1/2%) of the wholesale selling price of each printed copy and edition printed, published and sold in the United States and Canada by PUBLISHER or its licensees, for which payment has been received by PUBLISHER.

(c) Fifty percent (50%) of any and all net sums actually received by PUBLISHER (less any costs for collection) from the exploitation in the United States or Canada by the licensees of PUBLISHER of mechanical rights, electrical transcription and reproduction rights, motion picture and television synchronization rights.

(d) WRITER shall receive his public performance royalties directly from the performing rights to which he is affiliated (i.e. American Society of Composers, Authors and Publishers, Broadcast Music Inc.) and shall have no claim whatsoever against PUBLISHER for any royalties received by PUBLISHER from any performing rights society which makes payments directly to writers, authors and composers.

(e) Fifty percent (50%) of any and all net sums, after deduction of foreign taxes, actually received (less any costs for collection) by PUBLISHER in the United States from sales, licenses and other uses of the subject musical compositions in countries outside the United States and Canada (other than public performance royalties as herein mentioned in (d) above) from collection agents, licensees, sub publishers or others, whether or not same are affiliated with, owned or controlled by PUBLISHER.

(f) PUBLISHER shall not be required to pay any royalties on professional or complimentary copies which are distributed gratuitously to performing artists, orchestra leaders and disc jockeys or for advertising, promotional or exploitation purposes. Furthermore, no royalties shall be payable to WRITER of consigned copies unless paid for, and not until such time as an accounting therefore can be properly made.

(g) Except as herein expressly provided, no other royalties or monies shall be paid to WRITER.

Accounting: PUBLISHER shall compute the total composite royalties earned by WRITER on or before September 30th for the semi-annual period ending the preceding June 30th, and shall thereupon submit to WRITER the royalty statement for each period together with the net amount of such royalties, if any, as shall be payable after deducting any and all recouped advances and chargeable costs under this AGREEMENT or any other agreement between WRITER and PUBLISHER. Upon the submission of each statement, PUBLISHER shall have the right to retain, with respect to print sales as a reserve against subsequent charges, credits or returns, such portion of payable royalties as shall be necessary and appropriate in its best business judgment.

Entire Agreement. This AGREEMENT supersedes any and all prior negotiations, understandings, and agreements between the parties. Each of the parties acknowledges and agrees that neither party has made any representations or promises in connection with this AGREEMENT nor the subject matter hereof not contained herein.

COLLABORATION AND SEPARATE AGREEMENTS:

(a) Whenever WRITER shall collaborate with any other person in the creation of any musical composition, and such musical composition shall be subject to the terms and conditions of this AGREEMENT, WRITER agrees that prior to the collaboration, this person shall be advised of this exclusive agreement. In the event of such collaboration with any other person, WRITER shall execute a separate songwriter's agreement, setting forth the division of the songwriter's share of income between WRITER and such other person, and PUBLISHER shall make payment accordingly.

(b) If PUBLISHER so desires, PUBLISHER may request WRITER to execute a separate agreement in PUBLISHER'S customary form with respect to each musical composition hereunder. Upon such request, WRITER shall promptly execute and deliver such separate agreement and PUBLISHER shall have the right to execute such separate agreement in behalf of the WRITER. Such separate agreement shall supplement and not supersede this AGREEMENT. In the event of any conflict between the provisions of such separate agreement and this AGREEMENT, the provisions of this AGREEMENT shall govern. The failure of either of the parties to execute such separate agreement, whether requested by PUBLISHER or not, shall not affect the rights of PUBLISHER to all the musical compositions written and composed by WRITER.

Writer's Services: WRITER agrees to perform the services required solely and exclusively for and as requested by PUBLISHER. WRITER shall promptly and faithfully comply with all requirements and requests made by PUBLISHER. WRITER shall deliver a manuscript copy of each material composition immediately upon the completion or acquisition of such musical composition. PUBLISHER shall use reasonable efforts to exploit all compositions hereunder, but PUBLISHER'S failure to exploit any or all said compositions shall not be deemed a breach of this contract.

Unique Service: WRITER acknowledges that the services rendered hereunder are of a special, unique, unusual, extraordinary and intellectual character which gives them a particular value, the loss of which cannot be reasonably or adequately compensated in damages in any action at law, and that a breach by the WRITER of any of the provisions of this AGREEMENT will cause PUBLISHER great and irreparable injury and damage. WRITER expressly agrees that PUBLISHER shall be entitled to the remedies of injunction and other equitable relief to prevent a breach of this AGREEMENT or any provision hereof which relief shall be in addition to any other remedies for damages or otherwise, which shall be available to the PUBLISHER.

Governing Law: This AGREEMENT shall be governed by the laws and in the courts of the State of _____ and by the laws of the United States, excluding their conflicts of law principles. Any dispute or legal proceeding regarding the AGREEMENT shall take place in the county of _____, in the State of _____.

This AGREEMENT and option shall be considered renewed at the end of the period herein unless Artist receives a written notice with the intent to terminate this contract. Any questions relating to this agreement shall be interpreted in accordance with the laws of the State of _____.

Your signature below will constitute this as a binding agreement between us.

DATED: _____

AGREED TO AND ACCEPTED

_____
For Artist

_____
For Publisher

THE RECORDING MECHANICAL LICENSE

The last contract we will address will be one of the core documents of the publishing industry: the mechanical license. This is the license that the song owner, usually the publishing company, grants to record companies and artists for permission to record the song.

NOTE: You will have to provide proof of the mechanical license for each song on a CD when you send the CD to a reputable CD manufacturer. If you own the songs, grant yourself the license. If you are covering someone else's material you will have to include the mechanical you received from them when replicating.

When a song is created, it is owned by the writer or publisher. The rights for the first publication of the song are negotiable. If you have a killer song that Artist X's producer has just got to have, you can charge all the market will bear. The first recording is the only recording that you have this leverage with. All subsequent recordings (all the other covers of the song) have their mechanical rate set by law. Congress sets the statutory mechanical rate and it is adjusted upward on occasion to reflect inflation and other economic realities. The statutory mechanical rate at the time of this writing (March 2008) is:

9.10 cents for songs five minutes or less or 1.75 cents ($.0175) per minute or fraction thereof over five minutes.

For example:

5:01 to 6:00 = $.105 (6 × $.0175 = $.105)
6:01 to 7:00 = $.1225 (7 × $.0175 = $.1225)
7:01 to 8:00 = $.14 (8 × $.0175 = $.14)

You can check on the current mechanical rate by visiting harryfox.com—the largest mechanical clearing agency in the United States. In fact, it is far easier to pay a few dollars extra and pay your mechanical fees on the Web than going directly to the publisher via the mail.

As a writer or publisher, you could charge Artist X $5,000 for the right to first release and the statutory mechanical rate thereafter. So if Artist X is the first to release the song and makes 5,000

CDs, here's how the mechanical formula would work assuming the song is under five minutes in duration:

Initial First Release Fee:	Rights to First Release	$5,000.00
Statutory Mechanical Fee:	5,000 copies @ 9.10 cents	$455.00
Total for the First Run:		$5,455.00

Another point that bears mention before we look at the simple and brief mechanical license is that the statutory rate is the *ceiling* that the publisher or writer can charge. This does not mean that the publisher or writer cannot charge less. Situations sometime arise where a reduced mechanical rate is required to make a recording deal or overseas license work. In fact, when dealing with foreign markets expect to earn half of what you would in your home market. Major labels are famous for requesting or demanding a reduced mechanical rate unless, of course, they own the publishing.

RECORDING—MECHANICAL LICENSE CONTRACT

As you can see, the mechanical license is one of the simplest contracts you will find and if you use the Harry Fox online option, you plug in your credit card and the mechanical is produced as an Acrobat file you can print out.

Music publishing is a major component of the industry and now that we have something of a handle on the songs, let's take a look at the relationship between the songs, the artist, and our new friend the producer.

RECORDING - MECHANICAL LICENSE

This Agreement made and entered into this _____ day of 20__, by and between ___(Publisher)_____ (hereinafter referred to as the "Owner") and _____(Record Label)_____ (hereinafter referred to as the "Licensee").

Owner hereby grants to Licensee the right to record, reproduce, market and sell the musical composition now entitled:

under the following terms and conditions:

1.   Owner warrants and represents that it is the sole and exclusive proprietor of a valid copyright or license in the musical composition composed by:

(hereinafter referred to as the "Composition" or "Musical Composition"), and that Owner has the right to grant the license herein contained.

2.   Owner grants to Licensee the nonexclusive right, privilege and license, during the term of the copyright of said Composition and all renewals and extensions thereof, to use the Composition, and to make and/or use arrangements thereof, in the manufacture and sale of parts of instruments serving to reproduce the Composition in the United States.

3.   Licensee shall pay to Owner royalties at the following rates on all copies containing the above-named musical Compositions manufactured, sold and paid for in the United States during the term of the Composition's copyright and all renewals and extensions thereof:

(a)   For each phonorecord manufactured, sold, and paid for, the Licensee shall pay the Owner FIVE (5) CENTS.

(b)   The term "phonorecord(s)" or "records", as used herein, means any and all methods of mechanically reproducing the musical Composition including, but not limited to, phonograph records, CDs, DVDs, HD-DVDs, MP3s, cassette tapes, digital audio tape, compact disc and any and all methods of reproducing the Composition, now known or to later come into existence.

4.   Licensee agrees to render to Owner quarterly statements, and payments herefore, of all royalties payable hereunder, within 45 days after March 31st, June 30, September 30, and December 31, for each quarter for which any such royalties accrue pursuant to the terms hereof.

5.   (a)   As to records manufactured in the United States and sold by Licensee for export to other countries, royalties shall be payable pursuant to this contract, except with respect to records exported to countries which require the payment of copyright royalties in connection with the import or sale of such records, in which event no royalties shall be payable hereunder.

Page 1 of 2

(b)   As to all mechanical devices (such as masters, mothers and stampers) which are exported by Licensee to companies in other countries for use by such companies for the manufacture and sale of records, a royalty of ONE HALF the United States royalty rate shall be payable to the Owner.

6.   Owner indemnifies, and shall hold harmless, Licensee from loss or damage (a) arising out of or connected with any claim by a third party or parties which is inconsistent with any of Owner's warranties in paragraph 1 hereof, or (b) by reason of any adjudication invalidating the copyright of the Composition.

7.   This contract is assignable by either party as long as the royalty rate herein stated is paid to Owner and shall be binding upon the heirs, legal representatives, successors and assigns of the parties hereto.

AGREED TO and entered into by the parties hereto.

OWNER   **LICENSEE**

By _____   By _____

CHAPTER 8

Working with Producers

Bill Davis, Courtesy of The Music Office

The unsung heroes, at least to the listening public, of the music industry are the producers. The producer can wear many hats and have a major impact on an artist or band's career trajectory. There are different kinds of producers. Some producers are great musicians, writers, and arrangers in their own right. Many successful recording artists go on to be producers. On the other hand, there are producers that can't play a lick of music but know how to create, package, and sell a recording project. These producers, rather than being killer musicians, have a Rolodex full of great musicians and arrangers. Rather than focus on a particular riff, they are focusing on the overall groove, feeling and never take their eye off the prize. Both models can be successful.

Another aspect of a successful producer is that they have business savvy. Many producers know exactly what doors they will knock on when the mix is finished before they lay the first track.

If a producer is working a speculative deal, he may often become an equity- or royalty-based partner. Producers can work on both a speculative or royalty-based model or they can be brought in under a "work-for-hire" arrangement. The CD-ROM has examples of a number of producer scenarios from a basic artist/song deal to a film/television synchronization agreement. Let's look at a few of the more common platforms.

Work for Hire: In this scenario a producer is hired to complete a particular project with a certain artist within a certain time frame and on a budget. When the job is done, the producer walks away with no further interest in the recording or the artist. This method is preferred by smaller labels as it gives them a fixed cost rather than having to compute, report on, and pay further royalties to the producer. Many producers who normally get "points" in addition to their fees will do a fee-only based project as a favor or for an artist they are particularly fond of and want to associate with.

With Points: Producers with a track record of success will almost always be asking for points in the sale of the recording, particularly when dealing with the major labels. They are sometimes brought on by the label to develop a new act and their input can be regarded as the foundation for the sonic branding of the band. Producer points are not a very large piece of the pie, generally ranging from half a percent to three percent.

The Producer as Equity Partner: A producer can fall in love with an artist and decide to go way out on a limb and produce a master without any up front compensation. The producer will pay all the studio, musician, arranger, engineer, mastering lab, and other expenses of getting the artist's vision into a viable sonic product. This is a considerable expense and a producer will justly want to be compensated for it. In many scenarios the producer is grooming the act for a hand-off to a major label or management company. The producer has brought all the pieces together to make not just a recording but a product. With a great master in hand and the right relationship with the label, the producer has done all the work of the label's A&R department and in-house production. The producer delivers a turnkey product to the label, making their job easier, and will share in royalties paid by the label to the artist.

If it is indeed the producer that brings the artist to the record company's table, it is likely they will also want to share in a piece of the advance or other money that will be paid to the band by the label at signing and beyond. By making the introduction, the producer is taking an "agent" fee. It is conceivable, even likely for some producers, to be looking at three-fold income on one project. The money they are paid is for the actual production including the recording budget, a finder's or agent's fee for getting the band to the label, and a royalty on the recording produced. If a producer works a number of projects and stays busy over the years, this can be a very prosperous career.

You can mix and match components of these different production deals. Nothing is etched in stone and what may be applicable in one situation won't work for another. Don't forget that successful producers are artists and stars in their own right. They have managers, agents, and publicists too. They may not make the girls faint, but bands are sleeping on their doorstep in hopes of a shot.

In the next few pages we'll take a look at a short speculative deal that would have a producer paid a fee but also granted the right to shop the master exclusively to the major labels. The artist has already opened a dialog with a label, and this one label is off limits to the producer. The producer is compensated not only for producing but also if the master gets placed. At the end of this agreement (see page 93) you will also find a rider to the basic agreement. It spells out in greater detail what the producer will be compensated, both in production fees and royalties, whether the producer places the master or not. When an artist or manager executes this agreement, in terms of unit sales, the producer is now an equity partner.

PRODUCER'S LETTER OF AGREEMENT

Date:_____

Dear Mr./Ms. _____,
address

This letter shall serve as our agreement in respect to _____ (hereinafter referred to as the "Producer") services in producing Master Recordings (hereinafter referred to as the "Masters") of the recording artist(s) professionally known as _____ (hereinafter referred to as the "Artist").

1.   The term of this agreement shall commence as of the date hereof and shall continue until the completion of Producer's services.

2.   (a)   Recording sessions for the Masters shall be conducted by Producer under this Agreement at such times and places as shall be mutually designated by you and Producer. All individuals rendering services in connection with the recording of Masters shall be subject to your approval. You shall have the right and opportunity to have your representatives attend each such recording session. Each Master shall embody the performance by the Artist of a single musical composition designated by the Artist (subject to your approval, not to be unreasonably withheld) and shall be subject to your approval as technically satisfactory for the manufacture, broadcast and sale of phonorecords, and, upon your request, Producer shall re-record any musical composition   or other selection until a Master technically satisfactory to you shall have been obtained, provided additional production costs will be paid by you. Producer agrees to begin preproduction, rehearsals, and recording on _____, 20__.

(b)   Producer shall deliver to you a two-track stereo tape suitable for duplication and manufacture of phonorecords for each Master. All original session tapes, rough mixes and any derivatives or reproductions thereof shall also be delivered to you, or, at your election, maintained at a recording studio or other location designated by you, in your name and subject to your control.

3.   All Masters produced hereunder, from the inception of the recording thereof, and all phonorecords and other reproductions made therefrom, together with the performances embodied therein and all copyrights therein and thereto, and all renewals and extensions thereof, shall be entirely your property, free of any claims whatsoever by Producer or any other person or person engaged in the production of the Masters. (It being understood that for copyright purposes Producer and all persons rendering services in connection with such Masters shall be Contractors for hire).

4.   (a)   Conditioned upon Producer's full and faithful performance of all the terms and provisions hereof, you shall pay Producer, as an advance recoupable by us from any and all royalties payable by you to Producer hereunder, the sum of $ _____ DOLLARS payable upon commencement of recording, and the balance upon the delivery to you of the Masters.

(b)   Notwithstanding anything contained in (a) above to the contrary:

(i)   in the event the Masters are released on any label other than _____ or its subsidiary or affiliate label or labels, Producer shall not receive a royalty in connection with the sale of such records;

(ii)   in the event the Masters are released on the _____ label or a subsidiary or affiliate label, Producer shall be paid in respect to the sale of such phonorecords a royalty rate of three percent (3%) of the suggested retail price of each phonorecord sold and paid for in the United States. Payments of royalties from foreign sources shall be ONE HALF of the United States royalty rate. All fees paid to Producer hereunder shall constitute recoupable advances which shall be recouped prior to further payment of royalties.

5.   Producer has agreed to assist you in presenting the Masters to major record companies in pursuit of a record production agreement with a major label. Producer understands that you will also be presenting the Masters to major labels and that Producer will not be your exclusive representative. Therefore, Producer agrees to notify you prior to making any formal contact with representatives of any major record company on your behalf in order to coordinate our respective efforts and agrees to contact on your behalf only those companies we mutually agree upon. In the event you enter into a record production agreement with a major label for the Masters recorded hereunder and the further services of "Artist" as a result of substantial efforts and negotiations by Producer with such company within the period of ONE YEAR following the completion of the Masters we agree to pay you a commission of six percent (6%) of the actual cash advances (exclusive of recording budgets) received by you upon execution of said agreement. A major record company as defined herein shall be a company or corporation with gross sales of on million (1,000,000) units in the calendar year 2008.

6.   Producer hereby warrants, represents, and agrees that he is under no disability, restriction, or other incumbency with respect to his right to execute and perform the services described in this Agreement.

7.   You shall have the right, at your election, to designate other producers for recording sessions with the Artist, in which event Producer shall have no rights hereunder with respect to the Masters produced at such other recording sessions.

8.   We shall have the right, at our election, to assign any of our rights hereunder, in whole or part, to any subsidiary, affiliated, or related company, or to any person, firm or corporation acquiring rights in the Masters produced hereunder.

9.   (a)   This contract sets forth the entire understanding of the parties hereto relating to the subject matter hereof. No amendment or modification of this contract shall be binding unless confirmed in writing by both parties.

(b)   We shall not be deemed to be in breach of any of our obligations hereunder unless and until you have given us specific written notice of the nature of such breach and we have failed to cure such breach within thirty (30) days after our receipt of such notice.

(c)   Nothing herein contained shall constitute a partnership or joint venture between you and us.

(d)   This contract has been entered into in the State of _____, and its validity, construction, interpretation, and legal effect shall be governed by the laws of the State of _____.

(e)   This contract shall not become binding and effective until signed by you and countersigned by a duly authorized agent of ___(Company)_____.

If the foregoing correctly reflects your understanding and agreement with us, please indicate by signing below.

Sincerely,

_____
PRODUCER

Agreed and Accepted:

_____
ARTIST

ATTACHMENT A

ROYALTY PROVISIONS OF PRODUCER AGREEMENT

This attachment to the Producer Agreement between _____ (hereinafter referred to as the "Company") and _____ (hereinafter referred to as the "Producer") dated _____, 20__, is to specify the payment of royalties to Producer by the Company as follows:

1.   Producer has received EIGHT THOUSAND FIVE HUNDRED DOLLARS ($8,500.00) for his production of two Master Recordings of the Company's recording artist __(Artist)__. This is deemed as a recoupable advance against any royalties earned from sales.

2.   After the Company's recoupment of the above-mentioned advance, the Producer will be paid royalties at the following rate:

   (a)   For long playing 33 1/3 rpm phonorecords, CDs and any and all other methods of mechanically reproducing the performances embodied in the Master Recordings that are produced on the Company's label, its affiliate or subsidiary labels a payment of TWO AND TWO TENTHS CENTS (2.2) per copy thereof sold and paid for in the United States of America.

   (b)   For seven inch 45 rpm single releases or MP3 downloads which contain the Master Recordings produced by Producer a royalty of TWO AND THREE QUARTER CENTS (2.75) per side which embodies the Master Recordings produced by Producer.

   (c)   For any sales or license of the Master Recordings outside of the United States, a royalty of ONE HALF (1/2) of the United States royalty rate shall be payable on each copy that is sold and paid for and for which the Company has received payment in the United States. Royalty payments from such foreign sources shall be calculated at the rate of exchange at the time such foreign royalties are received by the Company in the United States.

3.   Royalty statements and payments shall be made semi-annually and will be made within 45 days of December 31st and June 30th of each year for the six month prior accounting period.

4.   Such royalty statements and payments to Producer shall be deemed to be final unless written notification by Producer to Company is made within one year specifying the reasons such statements and payments are unacceptable.

5.   Upon such written notice by Producer to Company, the accounting books of the Company which involve the Producer's royalties shall be made available to a certified public accountant designated by Producer.

6.   This Attachment is the sole basis for any and all payment of royalties by Company to Producer and supersedes and replaces any prior oral or written agreement between the Producer and the Company.

Understood and agreed to by the parties who have set their names below.

_____   _____
Producer   **Company**

CHAPTER 9

Working with Managers

Steve Seskin, Courtesy of The Music Office

There comes a point in a successful career where management is not an option, but a must. You will know when you get there. Your fans might be great at getting some posters up around town, but they won't find festival gigs, product endorsements, or know of other opportunities that are the lifeblood of a manager's career.

A manager makes his money on a percentage of the income he generates for his client. Management fees have ranged from as little as 15 percent to as much as the famous Colonel Parker/Elvis deal at 50 percent. The percentage that a manager can reasonably expect to receive should be based on how successful the manager has been in the past. An artist would be foolish to embark on a long-term relationship with an unproven manager. Newcomers to the management game have to prove themselves; and, as their success and notoriety grow, so does the percentage they can demand from their clients. Management agreements can be tied to performance where the manager's share goes up as earnings rise. This would be a must-have clause for a startup management person or firm if I was an aspiring artist.

When is it time to look into management? Ask yourself the following questions:

▶ Do I really need a manager?

▶ If so, for how long and for how much?

▶ What can a manager do for me that I can't do myself?

Managers work for money. No manager will last long in this business if they can't make a living. A manager may have to handle a number of artists to get to that place; or, if they are lucky, can make a living from managing just one artist—an artist that is earning about four times what the manager would like to take home. Let's look at it from a bottom-feeding viewpoint—the very basics of a management relationship. If you are looking for a manager that is going to focus solely on you, you will need to be earning quite a bit.

The Today Tones think they are on the way, the projections for this year look like a gross of over $65,000. Not bad for a band fresh out of the garage. The band might think it's time to look at management. Here's a look at what a manager would regard as perhaps not even a marginal situation.

Today Tones Worksheet—August 2008			
Income Source	Gross	Expenses	Net
Live Performance	$4,350.00	$265.00	$4,080.00
CD Sales	$450.00	$105.00	$345.00
Merchandise t-shirts	$385.00	$220.00	$165.00
All other income/expenses	$300.00	$83.00	$217.00
Total	$5,485.00	$673.00	$4,812.00

The band is netting about $4,800 a month. If this is the take for a group of weekend warriors, it's not a bad starting figure at all, but a manager looks at it differently.

Here is the manager's monthly take and yearly earnings based on different percentages of the manager's cut.

Manager's Band Assessment			
Group Name	Monthly Earnings	Manager @ 20%	Band Net
Today Tones	$4,812.00	$962.40	$3,849.60
		Manager @ 30%	
	$4,812.00	$1,443.60	$3,368.40

At the 20 percent rate, the manager will be earning about $11,500 a year, and at the upper limit rate of 30 percent the manager will pocket $17,300 before taxes. If your manager has any aspirations of the good life, you are going to have to do a lot better than $5,000 a month to get the manager's attention. If this manager had ten artists in his stable with comparable earnings to the Today Tones, he is starting to approach making a living. If the manager's goal was to earn a modest (in management's view) $150,000 a year and the Today Tones wanted his undivided attention, they would have to net $750,000 annually just to get the manager to this level at a 20 percent rate. If the band is more generous to the manager and pays 30 percent, they will only have to earn $500,000. Keep in mind these are *gross figures* that reflect income before any expenses are calculated.

Essentially, for the band to be really worth the manager's time and focus, they will have to grow their earnings by an almost ten-fold increase. Is the manager capable of making this happen? Is the band?

ARTIST MANAGEMENT AGREEMENT

Many other variables have not been put into play in this simple scenario and it is just an illustration of how the numbers might work. Let's drill down into a management agreement to see what the important points are including the attached Manager's Power of Attorney. The Artist Management Agreement on pages 98–102 shows what a performance-based simple management agreement might look like:

ARTIST MANAGEMENT AGREEMENT

AGREEMENT made this _____ day of _____, 20__ by and between _____(Artist)_____ whose address is _____ (hereinafter referred to as "Artist" and ___(Manager)_____ whose address is _____, (hereinafter referred to as "Manager").

WITNESSETH

WHEREAS, Artist wishes to obtain advice, guidance, counsel, and direction in the development and furtherance of his career as a musician, recording, and performing artist and in such new and different areas as his artistic talents can be developed and exploited; and

WHEREAS, Manager by reason of Manager's contacts, experience and background, is qualified to render such advice, guidance, counsel, and direction to Artist;

NOW THEREFORE, in consideration of the mutual promises herein contained, it is agreed and understood as follows:

1. Manager agrees to render such advice, guidance, counsel, and other services as Artist may reasonably require to further his career as a musician, composer, actor, recording, and performing artist, and to develop new and different areas within which his artistic talents can be developed and exploited, including but not limited to the following services:

   (a) To represent Artist and act as his negotiator, to fix the terms governing all manner of disposition, use, employment or exploitation of Artist's talents and the products thereof; and

   (b) to supervise Artist's professional employment, and on Artist's behalf, to consult with employers and prospective employers so as to assure the proper use and continued demand for Artist's services; and

   (c) to be available at reasonable times and places to confer with Artist in connection with all matters concerning Artist's professional career, business interests, employment, and publicity; and

   (d) to exploit Artist's personality in all media, and in connection therewith, to approve and permit for the purpose of trade, advertising and publicity, the use, dissemination, reproduction or publication of Artist's name, photographic likeness, facsimile signature, voice and artistic and musical materials; and,

   (e) to engage, discharge and/or direct such theatrical agents, booking agencies and employment agencies, as well as other firms, persons or corporations who may be retained for the purpose of securing contacts, engagements or employment for Artist; and,

   (f) to represent Artist in all dealings with any union; and,

   (g) to exercise all powers granted to Manager pursuant to Paragraph 4 hereof.

2. Manager is not required to render exclusive services to Artist or to devote his entire time or the entire time of any of Manager's employees to Artist's affairs. Nothing herein shall be

construed as limiting Manager's right to represent other persons whose talents may be similar to or who may be in competition with Artist or to have and pursue business interests which may be similar to or may compete with those of Artist.

3.   Artist hereby appoints Manager as his sole personal manager in all matters usually and normally within the jurisdiction and authority of personal manager, including but not limited to the advice, guidance, counsel, and direction specifically referred to in Paragraph 1 hereof. Artist agrees to seek such advice, guidance, counsel, and direction from Manager exclusively and agrees that he will not engage any other agent, representative, or manager to render similar services, and that he will not perform said services on his own behalf and he will not negotiate, accept, or execute any agreement, understanding, or undertaking concerning his career as an actor, musician, recording and performing artist without Manager's prior consent.

4.   Artist hereby irrevocably appoints Manager for the term of this Agreement and any extensions hereof as his true and lawful attorney-in-fact to sign, make, execute, accept, endorse, collect and deliver any and all bills of exchange, checks, and notes as his said attorney; to demand, sue for, collect, recover, and receive all goods, claims, money, interest and other items that may be due him or belong to him; and to make, execute, and deliver receipts, releases, or other discharges therefore under sale or otherwise and to defend, settle, adjust, compound, submit to arbitration and compromise all actions, suits, accounts, reckonings, claims, and demands whatsoever that are or shall be pending in such manner and in all respects as in any way limiting the foregoing; generally to do, execute and perform any other act, deed, or thing whatsoever deemed reasonable that ought to be done, executed, and performed of any and every nature and kind as fully effectively as Artist could do if personally present; and Artist hereby ratifies and affirms all acts performed by Manager by virtue of this power of attorney.

Artist expressly agrees that he will not on his own behalf exert any of the powers herein granted to Manager by the foregoing power of attorney without the express prior written consent of Manager and that all sums and considerations paid to Artist by reason of his artistic endeavors may be paid to Manager on his behalf.

It is expressly understood that the foregoing power of attorney is limited to matters reasonably related to Artist's career as a musician, actor, recording and performing artist and such new and different areas within which his artistic talents can be developed and exploited.

Artist agrees and understands that the power of attorney granted to Manager is coupled with an interest which Artist irrevocably grants to Manager in the career of Artist, in the artistic talents of Artist, in the products of said career and talents and in the earnings of Artist arising by reason of such career, talents, and products.

Simultaneously with the execution of this Agreement, Artist shall execute a short form power-of-attorney which Manager shall be entitled to file in any jurisdiction.

5.   (a)   As compensation for the services to be rendered hereunder, Manager shall receive from Artist (or shall retain from Artist's gross monthly earnings) at the end of each calendar month during the term hereof a sum of money equal to **ZERO PERCENT (0%)** of Artist's gross monthly earnings if such earnings are less than **TEN THOUSAND ($10,000.00)** dollars per month, **FIVE PERCENT (5%)** of Artist's gross monthly income if such monthly income is more than **TEN THOUSAND ($10,000.00) dollars and less than FIFTEEN THOUSAND ($15,000)** dollars per month, **TEN PERCENT (10%)** of Artist's gross monthly income if such income is more than **FIFTEEN THOUSAND ($15,000.00)** dollars and less than **TWENTY THOUSAND ($20,000)** dollars per month, **FIFTEEN PERCENT (15%)** of Artist's gross monthly income if

such income is more than **TWENTY THOUSAND ($20,000)** dollars per month, and Artist hereby assigns to Manager an interest in such earnings to the extent of said percentages.

(b)   The term "monthly gross earnings", as used herein, refers to the total of all earnings, which shall not be accumulated or averaged whether in the form of salary, bonuses, royalties, interest percentages, shares of profits, merchandise, shares in ventures, products, properties, or any other kind or type of income which is reasonably related to Artist's career in the entertainment, amusement, music, recording, motion picture, television, radio, literary, theatrical, and advertising fields, and Artist's artistic talents are developed and exploited, received from administrators, assigns, or by any person, firm, or corporation (including Manager) on his behalf.

    (i)   Royalty advances made to Artist which are deemed recoupable against future earnings by the party or parties making such royalty advances shall not be included in gross monthly income.

    (ii)   Royalty payments made to Artist after recoupment shall be payable to Manager at the scale and rate aforementioned in Section 5 of this Agreement.

(c)   The compensation agreed to be paid to Manager shall be based upon gross monthly earnings (as defined herein) of Artist accruing to or received by Artist during the term of this Agreement or subsequent to the termination of this agreement as a result of any services performed by Artist during the term hereof or as the result of any contract negotiated during the term hereof and any renewal, extension, or modification of this Agreement.

(d)   In the event that Artist forms a corporation during the term hereof for that purpose of furnishing and exploiting his artistic talents, Artist agrees that said corporation shall offer to enter into a management contract with Manager identical in all respects to this Agreement (except as to the parties thereto).

    (i)   In the event that Manager accepts such offers, then the gross monthly earnings of such corporation prior to the deduction of any corporate income taxes and of any corporate expenses or other deductions shall be included as a part of the Artist's gross monthly earnings as herein defined, and any salary paid to Artist by such corporation shall be excluded from Artist's gross monthly earnings for the purpose of calculating the compensation due to Manager hereunder.

(e)   In the event that Artist forms a corporation or enters into a contract with a corporation during the term hereof for the purpose of exploiting or furnishing his artistic talents, then in addition to any and all other considerations to be paid to Manager hereunder, Manager shall be entitled to purchase at least **TWENTY PERCENT (20%)** of the capital stock of such corporation at the price of **ONE DOLLAR ($1.00) PER SHARE.** Artist agrees expressly not to enter into any contract with a corporation for such purpose unless said option is made available to Manager.

(f)   Artist agrees that all gross monthly earnings as herein defined may be paid directly to Manager by all persons, firms, or corporations and may not be paid by such persons, firms, or corporations to Artist, and that Manager may withhold Manager's compensation therefrom and may reimburse himself herefrom for any reasonable and receipted fees, costs, or expenses advanced or incurred by

Manager that portion of Artist's gross monthly earnings which equals Manager's compensation hereunder and such disbursements incurred by Manager on behalf of Artist.

6.   Artist shall be solely responsible for payment of all booking agencies, fees, union dues, publicity costs, promotional or exploitation costs, traveling expenses and/or wardrobe expenses and reasonable expenses arising from the performance by Manager of services hereunder. In the event that Manager advances any of the foregoing fees, costs, or expenses on behalf of Artist, or incurs any other reasonable expenses in connection with Artist's professional career or with the performance of Manager's services hereunder, Artist shall promptly reimburse Manager for such fees, costs, and expenses.

7.   Artist warrants that he is under no disability, restriction, or prohibition with respect to his right to execute this Agreement and perform it's terms and conditions. Artist further warrants and represents that no act or omission by Artist hereunder will violate any right or liability to any person. Artist agrees to indemnify Manager and hold Manager harmless against any damages, costs, expenses, fees (including attorney's fees) incurred by Manager in any claim, suit, litigation, or proceeding instituted against Manager and arising out of any breach or claimed breach by Artist of any warranty, representation, or covenant of Artist. Artist agrees to exert his best reasonable efforts to further his promotional career during the term of this Agreement, and to cooperate with Manager to the fullest extent in the interest of promoting Artist's career.

8.   The initial term of this Agreement shall be for a period of ONE (1) YEAR with a FOUR (4) YEAR annual irrevocable option from the date thereof to renew this Agreement by written notice mailed to Artist no less than SIXTY (60) days prior to the expiration of the initial term or option periods, as the case may be.

9.   Manager agrees to maintain accurate books and records of all transactions concerning Artist, which books and records may be inspected during regular business hours by a certified public accountant designated by Artist upon reasonable notice to Manager.

10.   During the term of this Agreement, it is understood and agreed that there shall be no change or modification of this Agreement unless reduced to writing and signed by all parties hereto. No waiver or any breach of this Agreement shall be construed as a continuing waiver or consent to any subsequent breach hereof.

11.   It is agreed that as a condition precedent to any assertion by Artist or Manager that the other is in default in performing any obligation contained herein, the party alleging the default must advise the other in writing by Certified United States Mail of the specific obligation which it claims has been breached and said other party shall be allowed a period of SIXTY (60) days from the receipt of such written notice within which to cure such default.

12.   This Agreement does not and shall not be construed to create a partnership or joint venture between the parties hereto.

13.   (a)   This Agreement shall be construed in accordance with the laws of the State of _____ governing contracts executed and performed therein, and shall be binding upon and inure to the benefit of the parties, respective heirs, executors, administrators, successors, and assigns.

         (b)   The use of the masculine gender in this Agreement shall be deemed to include the feminine whenever the context shall so require.

IN WITNESS WHEREOF, the parties hereunder have subscribed their signatures in the day and year first above written.

by_____
  MANAGER

by_____
  ARTIST

SPECIAL POWER OF ATTORNEY

STATE OF _____   )

)

COUNTY OF _____   )

      I, _____(Artist)_____, City of _____, County of _____, State of _____, hereby appoint ___(Manager)_____, of _____, City of _____, County of __, State of _____, as my attorney in fact, to act in my name and in my behalf to execute contracts for my personal services as a performing artist and to perform all acts of whatever kind and nature as may be necessary or proper in the preparation and execution of said contracts and I agree to appear and perform said contracts.

in the event I do not appear and perform said contracts, and in consideration for _____ acting as my attorney in fact, I agree to indemnify _____ for any actual loss or damage to him including Court costs and attorney's fees, resulting from my failure to appear and perform said contracts.

      This instrument is to be construed and interpreted as a Special Power of Attorney whereby _____ is empowered to make valid and binding contracts for my personal services as a performing artist. The rights, powers, and authority of my attorney in fact, _____, to exercise any and all of the rights and powers herein granted shall begin on _____, 20__ and such rights, power, and authority shall remain in full force and effect until _____,20__ or until a written notice of termination signed by me is delivered to _____.

_____
Artist

DATED_____, 20__

Witness_____

Witness_____

A Power of Attorney will be attached to this type of contract to allow the manager to act in the artist's name. The form used for this purpose is shown on page 102.

Now I will explain certain things about the Artist Management Agreement that may not be clear.

Section 1: This paragraph describes what the manager is empowered to do in the name of the artist and it is comprehensive. The artist is turning all aspects of their career management over to the manager. The Manager's Power of Attorney, which will be a rider to the main contract, will codify this in front of a public notary. The manager also has to be reasonably available to the artist for career and business consultation. The manager has the hire and fire power, the ability to enter into agreement in the band's name. Obviously the manager is the professional on the team that will require the most trust as you are literally and legally placing your entertainment business future in their hopefully capable hands.

Section 4: This section continues to spell out management duties but also touches on what the artist cannot do. The artist has to direct any business inquiries or advances to the manager. There will be no moonlighting or working under the table in this agreement. The artist could be responsible for damages should such a violation occur.

Section 5: These paragraphs specify the compensation to the manager on a performance graded scale. An established and successful manager would probably require the deletion of this paragraph. If you are sitting in his office, it is a sign that you know what the manager's skills and rate are.

In the case of an artist or band trying out a manager new to the business, it might start the manager's commission scale to begin when earnings are increased. A band would look at the money they are currently earning as theirs. They made the contact, cut the deal and built the relationship before the manager came on line. This is a negotiable point for both agents and managers. The artist has a bit of wiggle room, but when it gets down to brass tacks, the manager will be taking over all the old accounts and many of them will fall by the way as the manager moves the band upwards in the pecking order.

Special Power of Attorney: This simple document will be needed by the manager to open bank accounts and take over the day-to-day business of the band. The manager will require the power to enter into enforceable, serious, and sometimes long-term agreements.

MANAGER SCHOOL

Managers have to start their careers somewhere and that somewhere might be your band. Many new managers are young, hungry, and capable, so a lack of experience is not always a bad thing. A new manager might see opportunity outside the box and exploit it. Unfortunately, most aspiring managers, like musicians, never get to the big game. This is why a couple basic cutout clauses are necessary for the band.

Changes to the contract to accommodate a new manager would first and foremost be performance based when talking about the manager's commission or cut. No performance, no payment. The manager has to take the band to increased earnings during a trial period or the contract is invalidated. Like a publisher paying for a song option to shop a song around, the new manager is given the tools they need but nothing more until they have proven themselves. Granting a power of attorney to a new manager might be something to wait on until some gauge of performance is assessed and a foundation of trust and rapport is established.

Having a manager will affect your bottom line immensely; not just in the manager's cut, but also in his expenses. Another negotiating hot spot is whether the manager gets paid his commission on gross or net earnings. It can make a major difference. If a band grosses $10,000 in a month and their expenses run $2,000, if the manager is keyed to the net income at a 20 percent rate they would earn $1,600 that month. If, on the other hand, the manager is tied to the gross earnings his commission base will be $2,000 for that month and his expenses are deducted from what is left or "below the line." If you take this simple formula and apply it to a band that is grossing millions annually, you can see why the small print in the management agreement can make a big economic difference.

Another one of the duties and responsibilities of the manager is to retain the services of other industry professionals. Let's take a look at who might be joining the team.

CHAPTER 10

Working with Indie Labels

Stratoslacker, Courtesy of The Music Office

The indie label is home to many emerging artists. Some of these labels are "boutique" labels that cater to a specific genre or type of act. Some of the more successful indie labels in recent years have focused on dance formats such as rap, trance, and hip hop. A number of these labels still sell their products on vinyl and their primary sales are to DJs and clubs for dance mixes. Another musical genre that has grown consistently over the last ten years is the Americana market. A quasi-genre of country, this format has brought a lot of great writers into the limelight. Americana artists require as much promotion and work as any other format, but the artist doesn't have to be dressed up as much as a mainstream push. Americana artists don't have to necessarily be pretty and they sure don't have to dance. The format has become a home to many writers who find the "Nashville Sound" a bit cliché and the Nashville struggle as not worth the trouble. A number of indie artists find regional success and can make a good living on it. After all, if you can sell 40,000 units in your region without the help of a major label, you will probably be hearing from them soon. That is their money you are earning!

The indies are generally owned and run by people close to the music and the artists—not the board meetings and spreadsheets. This can be both good and bad. An artist wants someone behind them who can see the value of the talent—a true believer. The owners of these indies work a release hard and depending on their connections and skills, may find some success. The downside to having a CEO who is passionate about the music is that to make an indie work you also have to have a CFO who is passionate about bookkeeping. Many small labels, even in this day of Quicken and MS Money, have terrible and sometimes nonexistent record keeping.

Any deal you sign with an indie, especially a startup should be of a short-term duration and have extension options that are open to both sides. Keep it simple and short. You don't want to sign a deal with what may soon be just a post office box.

Another thing that can shed some light on the bona fides and commitment of the indie is how they view the recording budget. In many cases the label will put up money to make a recording but the only people that don't appear on the payroll is the band. Let's become a fly on the wall at a meeting with Little Hit Records.

Label: We'll get you in the studio and cut this record. I have a feeling it will be big.

Band: What's the budget for recording, artwork, replication and promotion? How much money are we talking about?

Label: Without going into specifics, thousands of dollars. I have to pay the studio, the producer, the other musicians, the mastering lab, the replicators and work the release with hundreds of radio stations and DJs. Yes, it will be easily thousands.

Band: Don't we get any money for recording?

Label: We aren't Warner Bros. dude. I am trying to keep as much money in the war chest for promotion as possible. If I have to pay you guys, I have less money to promote with. Less promotion means less sales which means a smaller royalty paid to you guys. We sell decently and you will make plenty of money on the back end. This contract is royalty based. A label this size can't make cash advances against those royalties. It would bankrupt us.

Band: We are not talking about an advance, but a wage for being studio musicians. You said you were going to pay the engineer, studio, producer, and other musicians but nothing to us. Sorry if your commitment to the project doesn't extend to the band, we aren't interested. To make it easier for you though we will only charge the AFM demo recording rate instead of the master recording rate.

In my opinion, if anyone is going to be paid on a project, everyone should be. That doesn't mean that everyone gets paid the same, the producer or label will try to cut the best deal with each individual. But the bottom line is that if a label doesn't have the money to put forward an advance nor pay their artists for their recording time as studio musicians, it is also likely that the promotional war chest they are saving for will be similarly inadequate. In this scenario, I would tell the label to pay the fiddler if they want to dance. If everything goes south with the label, at least the artist was compensated as a session player for making a master recording. Even walking away from the deal can help your street credibility; "Did you hear? The Today Tones walked away from a deal with Mojo Management! They said the deal sucked!"

Regarding how much compensation a musician should receive in the studio for making these masters is again directly tied to the musician's savvy and mojo. A reasonable place to start your negotiations would be to ask for the same scale the local AFM union shop is requiring. I wouldn't advise cutting any tracks for less than at least the local union demo scale. If you are the small label, keep in mind that there is more than one reason to pay the artist the going rate. If the indie wants to assign this master to a major label or distributor, the indie will have to prove to the licensee that the session players were compensated enough that they won't be appearing in the future with monetary claims. The best way to assure this is to pay scale to people involved and have them sign off on the job they did and the compensation received. Paying scale also lets the artists in the community know that you are serious about the business of the business—not just a fan with a few extra bucks to throw at a band. Sometimes startup indies have to cut every corner possible to make things work, but the lion's share of their investment should be in development of the artist. Trying to get your artist to record on the cheap is not the best way to inspire loyalty or to nurture a long-term relationship.

Let's take a look at an indie deal that a producer, who also owned the label, put forward and was reworked by the artist's attorney by the time we get to this draft. There are a lot of legal issues that are unclear or dangling, but this deal will give you a good idea of how the terms of a contract can evolve from the initial offer. Read the following deal closely. It has strengths, but it is also flawed in some places. Can you find them?

RECORDING AND PERSONAL SERVICES AGREEMENT

Let's dissect this agreement (see pages 111–117) a bit and try to get into the heads of the participants. The beginning of the contract is mostly recitals, outlining who is who and what is being brought to the table.

Overall, this contract is a producer's shot at what is now becoming called a "360° Deal." We will be visiting these types of deals later, but as a quick explanation they are deals that go well beyond just a recording deal to encompass every aspect of the artist's career. It is a very common format for "boy bands" and other pop pabulum products. A producer gets a group of talented singers and dancers, finds some hit dance tempo material, builds an image and legend around each band member, and then cuts a hot dance record. Thus, the Village People or the Spice Girls are born. The producer is the band. The people you see on stage are puppets. The band did not pre-exist before the producer's vision. The producer can change band members at will.

Part 1—Term: This is where, from the producer's point of view, you want the longest term possible so that you have the largest window to recoup the investment and get it to pay off. The longer the term of the deal, the slower the ticking of the "your time's up" bomb. From the artist's side, it is of course the diametric opposite; you want to get in and out as quickly as possible. In an earlier draft there may have been extension options after one year, two years, etc.

Recording and Personal Services Agreement

This Recording and Personal Services Agreement, (hereinafter referred to as the "Agreement") executed and effective this __ day of _____, 20__, by and between _____ (Artist)_____ (hereinafter referred to as the "Artist") and _____(Company)_____ (hereinafter referred to as the "Company"):

Recitals

    a. Company is an organization which specializes in the management, recording, recording distribution and representation of musical artists;

    b. Company is familiar with the musical abilities of Artist and has the expertise, ability, industry contacts and resources to assist Artist in the furtherance of his/her career;

    c. Artist performs under the name "(Artist's Stage Name)";

    d. Company and Artist wish to enter into this Agreement to provide for the production and distribution of the Recording.

It Is, Therefore, Agreed as Follows:

A. Term. The effective date of this Agreement shall commence with its execution by all of the parties, and shall continue thereafter for a period of _____ (#) years.

B. Production of Recording. The Recording shall be produced in the following manner:

1. Production. Company agrees to produce one master recording consisting of songs written and performed by Artist (hereinafter referred to as the "Songs." The resulting recording (hereinafter referred to as the "Recording") shall include music of not less than forty-five (45) minutes in playing duration, and shall be of a quality which is equal to master recordings normally produced for commercial distribution.

2. Contribution by Artist. Artist agrees to fully cooperate with the Company, in good faith, in the production of the Recording; to contribute to such production the music and lyrics embodied in the Songs; to arrange, direct and perform the Songs in such a manner as to facilitate the production of the Recording; and to otherwise strictly observe the remaining duties and obligations of this Agreement.

3. Costs. Company shall be responsible for all costs incurred in the production of the Recording, including the prepayment of all travel, hotel and meal costs incurred by Artist in attending the recording sessions referenced in Section B.5 herein. Company may recover such receipted expenses pursuant to the production of master recordings or the advancement of the Artist's career. Company's production, promotion, manufacturing and all other bona fide expenses relating to Artist are deemed recoupable from gross income.

4. Artistic Control. Company and Artist shall be jointly responsible for all decisions regarding the artistic content of the Recording.

5. Dates and Location of Recording Sessions. The recording sessions necessary to produce the Recording shall occur at studios and facilities chosen by Company in __ (city, State) ____, commencing on _____, 20__ and ending on _____, 20__.

6. Additional Musicians. Company shall provide and compensate sufficient and competent musicians to properly perform the Songs, as arranged and directed by Artist and Producer. Company may recover such costs pursuant to Section B3. herein.

7. Title. The title of the Recording shall be chosen by agreement between the Company and the Artist.

8. Completion and Release.   The Recording shall be completed and prepared for release and distribution on or before _____, 20__. Company and Artist acknowledge that time is of the essence in the completion of the Recording, and each agrees to exercise all reasonable means to achieve such completion.

9. Assignment of Exclusive Rights by Artist. Upon the timely occurrence and performance of all material events and obligations required to produce the Recording, Artist shall assign to the Company all of his/her rights, title, and interest in and to the following property, for distribution and commercial exploitation in the United States and Canada:

      a.   The Songs,

      b.   Artist's performance of the Songs contained in the Recording,

      c.   The title of the Recording.

10. License for Use of Name and Image. Upon the timely occurrence and performance of all material events and obligations required to produce the Recording, Artist shall grant to the Company the exclusive license to use the name "___ (Artist) __", and the Artist's photographic image, in the promotion and distribution of the Recording.

11. Form of Assignment and License Documents. The form of ancillary documents to be executed by Artist, pursuant to this agreement shall be a publishing agreement (see Attachment A), an artist recording agreement (see Attachment B), and a personal management services agreement (see Attachment C) and are incorporated herein by this reference.

12. Copyright. Upon Artist's assignment of the Songs pursuant to Section 11. herein, Company shall proceed to obtain and secure a copyright for each of the said Songs. Each such copyright shall be the sole property of the Company.

13. Distribution. Commencing with the completion of the Recording and continuing for the term of this Agreement, Company will diligently use its best efforts to secure distribution of the

Recording throughout the world, through one or more major distribution companies (including record companies, film companies, or any other company). Any such contract entered into between Company and any such record distribution company shall be subject to the terms of this Agreement.

14. Royalties. In accordance with the rights granted by Artist to Company herein, Company intends to contract with a record distribution company for distribution of the Recording. Company will be entitled to receive royalties or licensing fees (herein collectively referred to as the "Royalties") as a result of such contract. Royalties shall include any compensation received by Company, or promised to Company, which directly or indirectly results from the use, exploitation or existence of the Recording, or any reproduction applied to satisfy costs incurred and paid by Company pursuant to Sections B.3, and B.6, herein. In the event that Royalties are insufficient to complete such reimbursement, Artist shall not be liable for such costs. The remainder of such Royalties, if any, shall be allocated and distributed between Company and Artist, in the following proportion:

   _____ (xx%)   **Percent to Company**

   _____ (xx%)   **Percent to Artist**

Royalties due Artist hereunder shall be delivered by Company to Artist within fifteen working days from the Company's receipt thereof.

15. BMI Membership. Within a reasonable time after the execution of this Agreement, Artist shall apply for registration and membership with Broadcast Music Inc. (BMI), a music licensing organization. Company shall be responsible for any cost or expense associated with such application or with the Artist's membership in BMI during the term of this Agreement and the Distribution Period. Company may recover such costs pursuant to Section 3. herein.

16. Non-Circumvention. Artist shall not detrimentally interfere with the efforts of Company to distribute the Recording through one or more distribution companies or enter into any contract inconsistent with the rights of distribution assigned to Company hereunder. Artist shall not contact any such potential distribution company except through the offices of the Company.

17. Additional Personal Services. For the term of this Agreement, Artist agrees to appear at one or more performances to promote the distribution of the Recording. Company shall schedule and arrange such performances, but Artist shall have the right of prior approval of the location, date and time of each such performance. The total number of performances during the term of this Agreement shall not exceed __ (# of performances) __. Company shall be responsible for travel, hotel and meal costs incurred by Artist in attending each such performance, Artist shall be paid one-half (1/2) of the net revenues received by Company for such performances. Such compensation shall be received by Artist within fifteen (15) days from Company's receipt thereof. Company may recover such costs (including travel costs and compensation paid to Artist) pursuant to Section B3. herein.

18. Option to Purchase. At any time during the term of this Agreement or thereafter, at Artist's option, Artist may purchase all rights assigned and/or granted to Company hereunder or resulting to Company herefrom (including rights of copyright to any and all of the Songs) for the total sum of:

       a. _____ (Amount (large) _____, plus;

       b. Any receipted costs expended by Company hereunder, but reimbursed, as of the date of exercise of such option to purchase, plus;

       c. _____ Percent (X%) of the gross revenues generated thereafter from the Recording. Exercise of the option shall be accomplished by the delivery of such amount, in cash or certified funds, to Company or its express designate. In the event of such exercise, Company shall promptly execute all documents reasonably necessary to effectuate such transaction. If and upon the exercise of such option, the obligations undertaken by the parties herein shall be exercised.

19. Assignment by Company. Prior to completion of the Recording, the rights and obligations of the Company existing hereunder are personal and unique, and shall not be assigned without the prior written consent of Artist. Subsequent to the completion of the Recording, Company may assign its rights and obligations existing hereunder without the consent of Artist.

20. Assignment by Artist. The rights and obligations of Artist existing hereunder are personal and unique, and shall not be assigned without prior written consent of Company.

21. Condition Subsequent. If Company does not enter into a binding contract for the distribution of the Recording during the Distribution Period, the assignment and license from Artist to Company granted pursuant to Section 11 herein and shall be deemed rescinded by the agreement of the parties.

22. Right of Inspection. At any time during the term of this Agreement upon prior written notice to Company of at least seven (7) days, Artist or his/her designated representative shall be permitted unrestricted access to the books and records of Company which in any way pertain to Artist, for inspection and photocopying by Artist or Artist's designated representative. Such books and records shall include, but shall not be limited to, any documents or records which evidence the receipt or disbursements of Royalties. Company shall maintain such books and records at its principal office.

23. Miscellaneous.

    a) Binding Effect. This Agreement shall be binding upon the successors and assigns of the parties.

    b) Arbitration. In the event of a dispute between Company and Artist regarding the terms, construction or performance of this Agreement, such dispute shall be settled by binding arbitration in _____(city, state)___, according to the rules of the American Arbitration

Association for the settlement of commercial disputes, then in effect. The award or decision resulting therefrom shall be subject to immediate enforcement in a __(state)__ court of competent jurisdiction.

(c) Jurisdiction/Applicable Law. Company and Artist hereby submit to the jurisdiction of the courts of __(state)__ for the enforcement of this Agreement or any arbitration award or decision arising herefrom. This Agreement shall be enforced or construed according to the laws of the State of _____.

(d) Attorney's Fees. In the event that a party is forced to obtain an attorney to enforce the terms of this Agreement, the party prevailing in such action of enforcement shall be entitled to the recovery of attorney's fees incurred in such action.

(e) Covenant of Good Faith and Fair Dealing. Company and Artist agree to perform their obligations under this Agreement, in all respects, in good faith.

(f) Independent Contractor. In the performance of his/her obligations of this Agreement, Artist shall be deemed an independent contractor

g) Incorporation of Recitals. The recitals contained at the beginning of this Agreement are incorporated herein by this reference.

Notices. Any notices or delivery required herein shall be deemed completed when hand-delivered, delivered by agent, or placed in the U.S. Mail, postage prepaid, to the parties at the addresses listed herein.

The Parties Agree to the terms and obligations and so execute on the day and date first above mentioned.

_____   _____

Artist   Company

Part 2, Paragraph 3—Costs: This is where the producer/ label states that their expenses are recoupable above the line at the gross income level. The reply appears to be that only receipted expenses will be recoupable. The label can't just pull a figure out of the sky.

Part 4—Artistic Control: This gives the decision on artistic matters equally to each party, but makes no stipulations about what happens at an impasse when artist and producer disagree. The same problem could arise when you look at Paragraph 7, another decision to be mutually made.

Part 9—Assignment of Exclusive Rights by Artist: This paragraph and its listing of the property to be assigned is murky at best. It could be construed by the producer/label as an assignment of publishing rights to the songs although the word "publish" doesn't appear in the clause. It is standard procedure for the producer/ label to own all the SR copyrights in a recording; that is the product securing the deal for them. But the publishing or PA copyrights are another thing entirely. Since this clause remained intact after review by the artist's lawyer I would hazard a guess that the artist's interpretation of it is that the producer was being granted exclusive mechanical rights only; not the songs themselves. Further down the contract in Paragraph 12 we run into the same problem. It specifies that the label will copyright the songs and will own the copyrights but it does not specify the form of copyright: PA, SR, or other type.

Part 14—Royalties: This is fairly standard for a percentage deal, which I strongly recommend against. It is much more favorable to be paid a small per-unit royalty than a percentage of net profits. From the artist's point of view, royalties are always best as viewed as an "above the line" item. Exorbitant expenses or padding of budgets by the label/producer can make "net" profits vanish into thin air. A compromise is conceivable and might be reached with the artist paid above the line on a per-unit basis, but on the backend below the line, although still sharing in a percentage of the net, this percentage would be reduced and added to the producer's column as putting the artist royalty above the line has increased the overall cost of the project.

Part 17—Additional Personal Services: This clause is also a little hazy. You can see the intent of the label to get the artist to appear at showcase gigs and promote the record. But specifying, "... one or more performances" doesn't quite say enough to me. From the artist's standpoint, if I saw the deal going sour I might perform one show and say, "The contract specifies one OR more. I chose the one option." Since the label is not looking for a piece of the gross receipts and is funding all the expenses, it would be unlikely to be construed that the label/producer wants to act as booking agent.

Parts 19 and 20—Assignments: A bit of protection, mostly for the artist, is in these two short clauses. Should the project not proceed to completion, the producer/label will not be able to assign any rights in the unfinished project to any third parties. This is important. It will almost certainly help see the project to completion as the producer's rights are based on this "all or nothing" stipulation. Should the artist agree to such assignment prior to completion, they can sign off on it. This could happen in the event the producer might be trying to assign the masters to an entity that could be even more beneficial and profitable to the artist. The artist has no rights to assign the master without written consent of the producer.

Overall, the standard definition clauses aside, this is a pretty weak deal and is something an artist or aspiring manager, producer, or label might see early on. It clearly states the intent of the deal but falls miserably short on specifics.

In our next example, we are going to look at another popular indie label product: the compilation album. If an indie has more than one artist on the label, they can cut down on promotional expenses by creating compilation albums that showcase the whole catalog instead of just one artist. They can service radio stations with samples of all their artists instead of a separate mailing and promotion for each.

Another common use for compilation albums is for charity fund-raising. Unsigned bands or bands on indie labels commonly will license one of their cuts to a charity for inclusion in a special fund-raising CD. An upside for the indie label is that even though the CD will have a limited life span (the length of the fund drive) it can lend to a new label's credibility to have multiple artists on one of their releases even if the artists are not signed to the label. The label gets a good release with little or no production costs. The label can pull the manufacturing costs off the top of sales (above the line) or donate the replication as a tax-deductible expense. The contract example on page 121 could be modified to fit this scenario easily.

RECORD MANUFACTURING AGREEMENT

Another possible source of income for the independent release is shopping the master in foreign markets. Many artists have found success in countries other than their home. Many American jazz artists cut their teeth in Europe before gaining any recognition on their home shores. Jimi Hendrix broke out of the U.K., not Seattle.

Shopping an overseas deal has become both easier and harder over the last two decades. With the advent of the E.U. (European Union), a master doesn't have to be shopped one country at a time. In the '80s when I would shop a master overseas for a client, I would try to place it in as many separate countries as possible. I might get a $4,000 advance for a master from a label in Denmark for the market of Denmark and another from France. That has all changed now that the borders are down. When you license to a European label they will now want the rights to the entire E.U. community—in essence, all of Europe.

Small labels make the trek to MIDEM in Cannes, France, the largest music licensing convention in the world every January to shop their wares to their foreign counterparts. Sometimes these sales trips wind up being buying trips if a small label sees an act with promise and wants to license the master for the United States. It can be a way to pick up a good master, again with no production cost but the promotional backend had better be in place or the license granted by the European label is likely to be rescinded.

The Record Manufacturing Agreement shown on pages 121–124 is an example of a contract used to broker foreign deals. There is the initial marketing agreement supported by attachments that describe the properties in detail and share other information like banking fees and the incentive for the publisher/writers to bless this licensing deal. Documents like this are used by MIDEM attendees to cover themselves when carrying and promoting products for their clients overseas.

RECORD MANUFACTURING AGREEMENT

AGREEMENT made as of the date signed below by and between _____ (hereinafter referred to as the "LICENSEE") and _____ (hereinafter referred to as the "OWNER"). In consideration of the following mutual covenants, conditions, and promises , the parties agree as follows:

I.   PURPOSE OF AGREEMENT

1.   Owner has recorded master sound recordings (Masters) of certain musical compositions. Either directly or by way of exclusive license, Owner has all rights, title, ownership, and interest, including copyright, in the Masters. Licensee does business throughout the United States and the world; which includes the manufacturing of recorded music and the publishing of musical compositions.

2.   Licensee desires to manufacture the Masters throughout the Territory.   With respect to the Master, the scope of the territory shall be worldwide, only for the purpose of a various artists sampler on a non-exclusive basis.

3.   This Agreement provides the terms by which owner authorizes Licensee to undertake that effort. The masters and compositions are identified in the attached exhibit, which by this reference is made a part of and an addendum to this Agreement.

VARIOUS ARTISTS-   **SAMPLER #1-**

II.   GRANT OF RIGHTS

1.   Owner licenses to Licensee, who in turn accepts the license, to undertake the following activities with respect to the Masters throughout the territory:

a.   The right to manufacture and sell phonorecords (including vinyl, tape, compact disc, and any other audio configuration now known or later developed of the Masters.

b.   The right to grant non-exclusive synchronization and performance licenses for the use of the Masters for profit in motion pictures, television films, and video productions produced in the licensed territory.

c.   All rights not expressly granted to licensee under sections a, b, and c in this, Article II, of this agreement are specifically reserved to the Owner.

d.   Owner warrants that he has the authority to grant Licensee the rights identified in sections a, b, and c of this Article II to commercially exploit the Master in the territory (worldwide).

e.   Owner further warrants that he is sole and exclusive owner of the ights to these Masters and has the power to enter into and uphold this Agreement and further warranties that the musical compositions of the Masters are new and original compositions and are not an infringement on the copyrights of any other and are not subject to any liens or other encumbrances.

III. RIGHTS AND OBLIGATIONS OF LICENSEE

Page 1 of 4

1.   Licensee agrees it will cause Owner's name to be printed on each copy of the masters that may be sold or distributed by Licensee as identified in the attached exhibit.

2.   Licensee will forward to the Owner at no cost ten (10) copies of each edition of the Masters that are published by the Licensee or under the Licensee's authority in each format (e.g. tape, vinyl, compact disc, sheet music, etc..) in which they are published and released for sale to the general public. Thereafter,Owner may purchase additional copies of the phonorecords or other formats at a wholesale price of _____ per unit.

3.   Licensee will, to the best of its ability, advertise,promote, and distribute and solicit for radio airplay, such Masters with the intention of promoting the musical artists represented herein.

4.   The Licensee shall prepare and compile the musical compositions onto one (1) record album and shall complete the production of said record album, including but not limited to, mastering, pressing, plating, titling, artwork, negatives and/or color separation, and assembly.

5.   The Licensee shall offer for sale the majority of copies of the Masters from the initial and subsequent pressings as sales and demand warrants; however no additional pressings shall be made after _____ months from the execution of this agreement without the express written consent of the Owner.

IV. RIGHTS AND OBLIGATIONS OF THE OWNER

1.   The Owner shall prepare and deliver to the Licensee within _____ days of the execution of this Agreement, a 1/4" 15 ips (without noise reduction) analog Master Tape Recording or a Digital Master Recording (e.g. Red Book Compliant CD, PCM, RDAT copies) with test tones of a quality and fidelity suitable for record reproduction or broadcast to be produced by the Licensee.

2.   The Owner shall pay to the Licensee the sum of _____ Dollars for production and promotion costs and expenses.

3.   The Owner shall notify in writing the Licensee of any additional licensing agreements that the Owner may enter into during the term of this Agreement as specified in this Agreement.

4.   The Owner agrees to supply the Licensee with complete copyright information and promotional material, including but not limited to, an 8" by 10" black and white photograph, the printed lyrics of the compositions, and any biographical material on the Owner that may be available. Owner hereby grants to Licensee rights to use such material in the promotion of the Masters.

5.   Owner agrees not to license the Masters to any other independent compilation album without the express written consent of the Licensee.

V. ROYALTY PAYMENTS

1.   The Licensee agrees to pay the following royalty shares to the Owner:

2.   As an advance against royalties payable to the Owner for the permission to manufacture, distribute, and sell phonorecords of the Master, Licensee agrees to pay the Owner a recoupable but non-returnable advance in the sum of $_____ (one dollar) and/or other good and valuable considerations.

3.   This advance payment is due upon the execution of this Agreement for the Masters identified in the attached exhibit. If Licensee does not place phonorecords of the Master for sale to the general public in the territory for reasons beyond its control or if the Licensee can not manufacture and distribute phonorecords of the Masters for reasons beyond its control, the advance specified in V(2) herein need not be returned to us by you.

4.   Payment of royalties resulting from licensing to foreign sources shall be one half (1/2) the royalty amount paid for the United States and Canada.

VI. ACCOUNTS AND STATEMENTS

1.   True and correct accounts by generally accepted accounting methods shall be kept by the Licensee and a statement of all accounts, including royalties due, if any, as of December 31 and June 30 of each year will be mailed to the Owner within sixty (60) days of these dates. All monies and reimbursements shown to be due under the terms of this Agreement shall be paid concurrent with the submission of said statement.

2.   All such payments shall be final and binding to Owner unless specific, written objection, stating the basis thereof, is submitted to Licensee by Owner within one (1) year from the date rendered. Owner or a certified public accountant in Owner's behalf, at Owner's expense, and at reasonable intervals, may examine the Licensee's books relating to the activities during the accounting period for said account statement with written advance notice served by U.S. mail at least ten (10) days prior to such inspections or audits.

VII. TERM OF AGREEMENT AND COPYRIGHTS

1.   The Term of this Agreement shall be for the life of the copyright of the recording of said Masters and any and all extensions as per Form SR of the U.S. Library of Congress.

2.   Despite the expiration of this Agreement without renewal after the end of this term, Licensee nevertheless shall be obligated to make payments to Owner of any and all unpaid royalties still accruing on the Masters and compositions subsequent to its expiration.

3.   The term of this licensing Agreement shall be a period of five (5) years with an open option period for both Licensee and Owner of an additional five (5) years.

VIII. ENFORCEMENT OF COPYRIGHT

1.   Owner authorizes and vests power of attorney to the Licensee to enforce and protect in the territory all of the rights to the Masters and compositions licensed under this Agreement and, if necessary, to join Owner and such others as it deems advisable in any suit or litigation concerning the enforcement of such rights.

2.   Any damages or recovery awarded the License by the courts against any infringer shall be divided equally between the Owner and the Licensee, after the deduction of all costs incurred in such litigation.

IX. TERMINATION

1.   After the expiration of this Agreement, Licensee shall have the right to sell the remaining inventory. Licensee shall continue to deliver to the Owner royalty statements and payments as outlined in this Agreement accordingly.

2.   After the expiration of this agreement, Licensee shall deliver to Owner a written inventory of the phonorecords of the Masters that have not been sold. If Licensee does not wish to

continue to sell to the general public the remaining inventory, Owner shall have the right to buy the phonorecords at wholesale plus shipping.

X. EXCLUSIVITY

1.   Owner grants to the Licensee the option to acquire the rights to manufacture the licensed Masters worldwide on the basis of a "matching offer option". As soon as the Owner receives an offer from a third party for a license of the Masters in any of the territory, he has to inform the Licensee with the details of such an offer in writing.

2.   Licensee has the option to acquire said rights providing he is willing to offer the same contractual conditions as the third party. Licensee will not be required to agree to any conditions which cannot be fulfilled by Licensee as readily as by any other party.

XI. GENERAL

1.   This Agreement shall be binding on the respective parties, their successors, and assigns and shall be governed by and interpreted in accordance with the laws of the State of _____. The place of jurisdiction shall be _____ County, __(state)__ for any possible, dispute, suit or litigation arising from this Agreement.

2.   This Agreement contains all the understandings, oral and written, of the parties and merges all previous agreements.

3.   If any portion of this Agreement is found to be invalid or unenforceable, it shall not affect the balance of this Agreement.

Entered into and agreed upon this _____day of _____,20__ .

_____Licensee

_____Owner

INTERNATIONAL MARKETING AGREEMENT

Another way that indie labels can cut costs is to co-promote products and events. If you can get other like-minded businesses or sponsors to share some of the promotional costs, you can both save money and perhaps nurture a longer term relationship. Rights to market and promote the product are assigned to a third-party vendor in an effort to widen markets. You could modify Paragraph 3 to state that this deal could be for the specified initial term. And, if everything works out to the satisfaction of both parties, a renewal can kick in.

International Marketing Agreement

An Agreement made this _____ day of _____, 20__ between
_____(Agent)_____, _____(address)_____, (hereinafter referred to as the "Agent") and _____,of _____, USA (hereinafter referred to as the "Client").

The Agent hereby agrees to market _____ copies of the Client's audio product, listed in the attached "Exhibit A" (hereinafter referred to as the "Product"), to the Agent's foreign outlets under the following terms and conditions:

1. The Client agrees to pay in advance to the Agent the sum of _____ Dollars per copy of the product as a non-refundable retainer for the Agent's services in marketing the Product to territories outside of the United States of America.

2. The Client warrants to the Agent that the Client owns or controls the master recording, artwork, and all rights and copyrights relevant to the Product. The client shall inform the Agent of any and all territories where sub-publishing and/or licensing of the Product have been reserved; and in the cases where sub-publishing and/or licensing have not been reserved, the Client warrants that foreign sub-publishing and/or licensing rights to the Product are available. In addition, the Client warrants that the Product is not bound by any other contractual obligation which would preclude the Agent's fulfillment of any and all terms or parts of this Agreement.

3. The Agent shall be the exclusive representative of and for the Product to any and all territories outside the United States of America for an initial period of three (3) months, commencing the date that this Agreement is executed. The Agent reserves the option to extend this period for three (3) additional consecutive terms of three (3) months each to facilitate pending agreements. The Client must be informed of the exercise of the foregoing Agent's options in writing, sent prior to the expiration of the initial term. Such notice shall identify the third parties wherein possible agreements are pending and the territories to be covered.

4. The Agent shall provide to the Client monthly progress reports on the Agent's efforts on behalf of the Client.

5. In the event any outlet responds positively to the Product, the Agent shall inform the Client immediately, since the Agent is not empowered to enter into any negotiations on the Client's behalf without the Client's prior consent. If such event(s) occur(s) and a contract is made, the Agent shall receive a share as defined in "Exhibit A" and the Client shall receive the remaining share, also defined in "Exhibit A" of all advances, royalties, and other revenues received in the United States of America from territories outside the United States of America including publishing income, but excluding writer's income, as a result of such contractual agreement(s) secured for the Product directly or indirectly by the Agent on the Client's behalf. All offers and contracts shall be forwarded to Client for his review and commentary in negotiations.

6. For each contractual agreement secured by the Agent on the Client's behalf, the Client agrees to supply all necessary production parts at the Client's own expenses, and to reimburse the Agent

for reasonable telecommunication, postage and freight expenses incurred in the pursuit of bona fide offers to contract with Client.

7. Any and all contractual agreements secured by the Agent on the Client's behalf shall extend the term of the Agent's exclusive representation of the Product in the territory(s) in which the Product is contractually bound for a period equal to the term of such contractual agreement(s) including any and all options, renewals, and extensions set forth in such agreement(s).

8. The Client shall, for a period of twelve (12) months from the date this Agreement is executed, afford the Agent the right of first refusal to negotiate contracts regarding assignment of the Product within the territory of the United States of America if such negotiations have arisen as a direct result of the Agent's endeavors outside the United States of America. The Client further agrees to pay the Agent a share as defined in "Exhibit A"' of all advances, royalties, and other revenues originating in the United States of America including publishing income, but excluding writer's income as a direct result of negotiations by Agent in and for the territory of the United States of America. Furthermore, if in the case that the Client selects to have the Product represented in the United States of America by a party other than the Agent, then the Client shall pay the Agent a share, defined as one-half (1/2) of the Agent's share, defined in "Exhibit A", of all advances, royalties, and other revenues originating in the United States of America including publishing but excluding writer's income from any contractual agreement in and for the territory of the United States of America which arises as a direct result of the Agent's endeavors outside the United States of America.

9. The Client reserves the right to examine and negotiate, accept or reject directly, or through Client's legal representative, any contractual agreement(s) between third parties and the Client regarding the Product before such agreement(s) is entered into.

10.

    (a) Agent and Client agree that all contractual agreements secured under the terms of this Agreement shall be made in the name of ___(Owner) _____ with _____(Agent)_____ as "Agent". Furthermore, all financial instruments containing advance and/or royalty payments associated with such agreements shall be made payable to " _____(Agent / Owner)____" and shall be deposited in escrow at: [Name and Address of Bank] (hereinafter referred to as the "Bank").

    The escrow account at the Bank shall be named "__(Client and Agent) _____". The Agent and the Client agree to appoint and authorize ____(Agent)_____ to endorse, on behalf of Agent and Client with his signature and the phrase "for deposit only," all financial instruments made payable to "_____(Agent and Client)____" and deposit such instruments into the escrow account.

    (b) The Agent and Client authorize the Bank as escrow agent to collect and hold all monies deposited in said escrow account until it is instructed in writing jointly by the Agent and Client to divide the monies in accordance with the percentages set forth in "Exhibit A" and to distribute simultaneously the respective shares to the Agent and Client.

(c) The fees for the Bank's services for acting as escrow agent in these regards shall be deducted before any distributions are made and are listed in "Exhibit B." The distributions shall come from the net proceeds thereafter.

(d) The Bank shall act as escrow agent only. Both parties to this agreement agree to hold the Bank harmless for any claims or charges that either party feels it may have against the other or that any outside third party may have against the Agent and/or Client.

11. The Agent shall forward to the Client all royalty statements, source documents, and copies of correspondence and escrow statements received within thirty (30) days of receipt of same.

12. The Agent and the Client agree that all financial transactions between the Agent, the Client, and any of the Agent's foreign outlets shall be transacted in U.S. dollars computed at "the source."

13. The Client indemnifies the Agent from any legal claims regarding the Product not associated with this Agreement. The Client understands that he has purchased a marketing service and as such the Agent can make no guarantees with regard to the successful conclusion of any contractual agreements.

14. Failure of Agent to account as provided herein shall give Client the right to terminate this Agreement on 30 days written notice.

15. This Agreement shall be construed under and governed by the laws of the State of __(state)__ applicable to contracts made, executed and performed therein. If any portion of this Agreement is found to be invalid or unenforceable, it shall not affect the balance of this Agreement.

16. Nothing herein shall be construed to create a partnership or joint venture.

17. The Client retains all ownership of any and all rights of copyright in the Product.

The Parties to this Agreement indicate by their signatures below that they agree to and will abide by the terms of this Agreement.

_____   _____
            Client   Agent

by _____   by _____
          Title   Title

Date: _____, 20__.

Exhibit "A"

This document serves as "Exhibit 'A'" to the International Marketing Agreement between _____(Agent)_____ and _____ made this _____ day of _____, 20__.

The product(s) subject to the above is listed below, with the relevant shares of income as defined in the terms of said Agreement.

Product Agent's Share Client's Share

Includes the Following:

Artist: _____

Titles:

1.
2.
3.
4.
5.
6.
7.
8.
9.
10.
11.
12.

Published by _____

Exhibit "B"

This document serves as "Exhibit 'B'" to the International Marketing Agreement between

_____(Agent)_____ and _____ made this ____ day of

_____, 20__.

The following is a list of bank services relevant to the escrow account provided for in Paragraph

9 of the Agreement. This information has been supplied by _____ (Bank) _____, of

_____Address __, __State__.

Schedule of Services (Effective _____ 20__)
1. Monthly Maintenance fee (business checking account)* $ 4.00
2. Collection Items ** $ 15.00
3. Transfer of Funds between Accounts $ 20.00
4. Cashier's Check $ 5.00

Notes:
 * The account will actually open when the first item is deposited. No checks will be printed for this account.

 ** Collection Items are defined as instruments drawn on foreign banks. Any items deposited in the account which are drawn on U.S. banks will be charged at six cents ($0.06) per item and will be subject to hold until actually collected.

Writer's/Publisher's Inducement

As a material inducement to _____(Writer/Publisher)___ for entering into the International Marketing Agreement between Agent and ____(Owner)_____ dated this ____ day of _____, 20__, and knowing that _____(Agent)____ will rely thereon, I(We) _____, doing business as _____ hereby warrant, represent and agree that:

    (a) I(We) have read the above-mentioned agreement;

    (b) I(We) have granted to _____, for the purposes of the above-mentioned agreement, the control and use of all rights to all copyrights ("titles"), in my(our) songs/publishing catalogue and its successors or assigns, including but not limited to those titles listed in Exhibit "A" said Agreement, necessary to empower _____ to enter into the above-mentioned Agreement with Agent. (Refers to Paragraph 2);

    (c) Agent shall have the benefit of all agreements, warranties, representations and indemnities made by me(us) to _____ with respect to the titles;

(d) I (We) accept and agree that the Agent shall be entitled to share in any publisher's income as a result of Agent's efforts, at the percentage rate defined as "the Agent's Share" in Exhibit "A" of the above-mentioned agreement. (Refers to Paragraphs 5 and 8);

(e) I (We) agree to be bound by the aforementioned agreement to the extent same relates to me(us); and

(f) I (We) shall look solely to _____ for any amounts due me (us) in respect of any and all exploitations of the titles.

Agent may proceed against me(us) directly for any breach of the foregoing representations, warranties, and agreements without first or concurrently pursuing any remedy Agent may have against _____ or any other person. No alteration, modification, or amendment of the foregoing agreement shall affect Agent's rights or my(our) rights and obligations under this inducement.

Signed this _____ day of_____, 20__.

For_____

By _____ Title _____

CO-OP PROMOTIONAL AGREEMENT

Another method of skinning the same cat is to license the product totally and exclusively instead of working an alliance similar to the contract above. If the licensee has better public visibility, distribution, and more points of sale, this could take a lot of the weight off the small label or management team. The merchandising of all or portions of the artist catalog would be handled exclusively by the licensee and usually for a much longer period of time than would be assigned to a co-promotion. Similar to management, agents, and publicists agreements, certain rights beyond the product such as logos, images, and such also have to be conveyed to allow the licensee to promote and market the product. Let's peek into a merchandise licensing deal.

CO-OP PROMOTIONAL AGREEMENT

This Co-Op Promotional Agreement ("Agreement") is made and effective this __ Day of _____, 20__ by and between _____ (hereinafter referred to as the "Reseller") and _____ (hereinafter referred to as the "Vendor").

Vendor sells products under the trade name _____ (the "Product"). Reseller resells and/or promotes the sale of many goods.

Vendor and Reseller desire to arrange for Vendor to supply the following materials and pay to Reseller for Reseller's promotion of the Product as set forth herein.

NOW, THEREFORE, it is agreed:

1.   Product Promotion. Reseller agrees to provide the following special promotion of the Product (the "Promotion"): [Promotional Activity]. Reseller will take all necessary steps to make sure that the Promotion is timely and completely carried out by doing one or more of the following, as appropriate: Personally delivering through messenger or other service to each of Reseller's selling locations or outlets the promotional material, informing local managers that Vendor's personnel will be present to provide additional training and or support, and the dates of the training and support; confirming with local managers that Reseller's obligations are being timely completed. If the Promotion involves placement of Vendor's advertising in a catalog, tabloid or circular insert, Reseller shall insure that such advertisement or insertion, if any, is made exactly as specified in this Agreement.

2.   Materials.

        A.   The following materials are provided by Vendor upon execution of this Agreement or will be provided shortly to enable Reseller to timely complete the Promotion: [Materials Provided by Vendor].

        B.   The following material is in the possession of Reseller and will be used by Reseller n performing the Promotion: [Materials Provided by Reseller].

3.   Term. The Reseller will completely implement the Promotion not later than _____ and the promotion shall continue until _____.

4.   Principal Contacts and Notices. The principal contact for each party for the purpose of discussing matters related to this Agreement is as follows:

        If to Reseller:

        _____
        _____
        _____

        and if to Vendor:

        _____
        _____
        _____

Any notice given pursuant to this Agreement shall be in writing to the individuals identified above by overnight delivery service.

5.   Proof of Performance. Reseller shall provide Vendor reasonable proof that the Promotion has been completed on a timely basis including, but not limited to the following evidence: [Reseller Proof].

6.   Fees & Charges. In consideration of the performance of the Promotion as set forth herein, Vendor shall pay Reseller $_____. Vendor shall pay the fee to Reseller not later than thirty (30) days following Reseller's' delivery to Vendor of proof of performance as set forth in Section 5 above together with Reseller's invoice. Reseller is not entitled to deduct the amount of its fees for the Promotion from amounts to be paid to Vendor for Product purchases or any other charges. In the event of a good faith partial performance by the Reseller, Vendor shall pay Reseller a pro rata portion of the fees, but only if Reseller has substantially completed its obligations in this Agreement.

7.   Use of Marks. Vendor hereby grants to Reseller a limited right and license to use Vendor's name, logo, and trademarks (the "Marks") associated with the Product to perform Reseller's obligations in this Agreement. Use of the Marks is subject to Vendor's prior approval. Reseller's license in the Marks shall terminate upon the conclusion of the Promotion.

8.   Complete Performance. In the event that Reseller fails to supply adequate proof of performance, or if Reseller has not substantially completed the Promotion for the benefit of the Vendor as set forth in this Agreement, then Vendor shall not be obligated to pay any part of the fee to Reseller. In such event, Vendor may offer to Reseller its next available similar promotional opportunity which Reseller may accept or reject at its own discretion.

9.   No Waiver. The waiver or failure of either party to exercise in any respect any right provided in this agreement shall not be deemed a waiver of any other right or remedy to which the party may be entitled.

10.   Governing Law. This agreement shall be construed and enforced according to the laws of the state of _____.

11.   Headings. The section headings used in this agreement are provided for the convenience for the parties only and shall not be used to construe the meanings or intent of any term.

IN WITNESS WHEREOF, the parties hereto have caused this agreement to be executed as of the date first written above.

_____   _____
Reseller   Vendor

Date: _____   Date: _____

Merchandise Licensing Contract

This Agreement is for the services of music and/or entertainment described below between the undersigned Owner and the undersigned Licensee. Owner creates and produces CDs, cassettes, videos, and sheet music, hereinafter referred to as "Music Products". Licensee provides manufacturing, marketing and distribution facilities for products in the Licensed Territory referred to below.

1. Owner hereby grants to Licensee the exclusive and non-assignable rights to manufacture, sell, and distribute music products detailed in Exhibit A, without limitation or restriction, anywhere in the territory of the United States of America (herein called "Licensed Territory") for a period of _____ years from the date of this agreement.

2. All other rights regarding the aforementioned musical products are reserved by Owner, except as provided for in this agreement.

3. Owner may elect to cancel or terminate this agreement for the following reasons:

> a. If Licensee fails to account and make payments or fails to perform any other obligations required and such failures are not cured within thirty (30) days after written notice to Licensee;
> b. In the event that Licensee is forced to liquidate or file bankruptcy.

4. Licensee agrees to pay Owner a sum equal to twenty two and one half percent (22.5%) of gross funds received by Licensee in the Licensed Territory. Licensee shall notify Owner of gross funds received within thirty (30) days from the date thereof, and will notify Owner of any changes within fourteen (14) days. In the event payment due to Owner is delayed or denied by governmental regulations, Owner shall designate a local depository in the Licensed Territory in which Licensee shall deposit these funds.

5. Royalties due to Owner shall be made on a monthly basis and shall be accompanied by a detailed statement listing the number of records sold from each master, as well as all charges, royalties and claims. All payments made by Licensee shall be computed in local currency effective on the payment date, subject to any governmental exchange regulations in effect.

6. The royalties paid by the Licensee to the Owner are intended to include provisions for all recording artists and other talent, paid entirely by Owner. Licensee shall be free of any obligations to pay the costs of the recording sessions.

7. With respect to musical products manufactured or sold from master recordings which embody copyrighted musical or other material, Licensee agrees to pay all royalties which may be due to proprietors of the copyrights (or duly authorized agent).

8. Licensee agrees to begin the manufacture and sale of recordings within three (3) months from the date of this agreement. In the event Licensee fails to do so, all rights

Page 1 of 5

133

granted shall automatically cease and terminate.

9. Licensee agrees that all records manufactured by and under this agreement shall bear the imprint of the following words on the label, album cover and/or sleeve:
"_____ (Artist), Used by Permission."

10. Licensee agrees to defend, indemnify and hold Owner harmless against any and all liability, loss, damage, cost or expense, including attorney's fees, paid or incurred, by reason of any breach of any covenants, warranties, or representations.

11. All musical products shall be released in their entirety, without editing and for the purpose originally recorded by or for Owner, unless Owner provides written consent. Adaptations by Licensee for different record speeds shall be deemed authorized. Licensee shall couple performances in a CD, record, cassette, video and music book only in the same manner as the master recordings manufactured by the Owner and only the compositions contained in masters supplied by Owner, unless otherwise notified in writing by Owner. Recordings shall not be supplied by Licensee to record clubs, nor for promotional giveaways or other devices for mass distribution without receipt of payment, without Owner's prior consent in writing. Advertising or disc jockey promotions shall be deemed exempted from the foregoing prohibitions.

12. Owner agrees to deliver master recordings by supplying to Licensee one or more duplicate tape recordings, or duplicate of the sheet music originals, at Owner's cost price plus any actual expenses incurred for packing and shipping (including insurance). Such tapes and masters shall be delivered to Licensee as promptly as possible following the submission of written orders to Owner.

13. At the time of the delivery of the first such derivative from each master recording to Licensee, Owner shall supply the following to Licensee, in writing:

> a. the correct title of the recorded work;
> b. the names of the author, composer, and publisher, together with any additional copyright information known to Owner;
> c. the names of the recording artists as Owner displays or intends to display them on the labels of the products marketed by Owner.

14. With respect to master recordings delivered, Owner agrees to supply to Licensee samples of its advertising and promotional materials including catalogues, supplements, release sheets, liners, photographs of artists, and the like, which shall be delivered to Licensee from time to time for use in the United States of America. All such samples will be free of charge, except that Licensee will pay all expenses for packing and shipping (including insurance), customs, duty fees and expenses. Licensee shall have the right to use all or any part of such material, in its original form or with minor modifications. Owner agrees, upon request, to supply to Licensee any such material in quantity, or plates for reproducing the same, at Owner's cost plus any actual expenses for packing and shipping (including insurance). Owner may require that such payments be made by sight

draft against bill of lading. Licensee shall have the right, at its option, to reproduce any or all such material for use provided that Owner itself has obtained the right to grant such right to Licensee and Licensee shall have made any payments necessary in such connection.

15. The rights hereby granted by Owner to Licensee are the following:

> a. The right to manufacture, sell, publicly perform, and advertise records containing the performances embodied in the master recordings in the Licensed Territory only;
> b. The right to use name, likeness, and biography of each artist whose performance is embodied in the master recordings for advertising, publicizing or sale of musical products in the Licensed Territory, provided that Licensee shall abide by any restrictions imposed upon Owner.

16. Licensee shall supply Owner with a minimum of _____ sample copies of each release.

17. Licensee shall make available to Owner copies of each release as follows:

> a. Unlimited copies at the Licensee's cost for the Owner's purpose of promoting concert, television, and radio performances as well as other promotional purposes. These copies shall not be sold to the public, nor shall they be given to the public free of charge.
> b. Unlimited copies at 40 percent of the suggested retail price, for the Owner's purpose of selling to the public after concerts, performances and programs and at the _____ retail location. It is understood that Licensee shall still remit to Owner the 22.5 percent royalty on the gross received for these purchases as specified in Paragraph 4.

18. All masters and duplicates of recordings and compositions, and all copyrights, ownerships and rights in and to such recordings, shall remain the sole and exclusive property of Owner, subject to the rights of Licensee to make reproductions pursuant to the terms of this agreement.

19. Owner shall have the right to inspect and make extracts of the books and records of Licensee, its subsidiaries, affiliates, licensees and assigns. Such inspections shall be made with ten (10) days written notice, during normal business hours, but not more than once annually.

20. Licensee agrees to sell recordings manufactured only in the normal course of business and at regular prices. Licensee shall refrain from distress and closeout sales of such recordings.

21. Upon the expiration or other termination of this agreement, all pressing and printing by Licensee shall cease. Regarding all masters, including any made by Licensee, and any

other material in Licensee's hands used in the manufacture of Owner's records, Licensee shall promptly, at the option of the Owner and upon its written instructions, either:

a. deliver same to Owner in the United States of America or Licensed Territory, as designated by Owner at Owner's sole expense of delivery,
b. transfer same at Owner's sole expense of delivery to any other company designated and approved by Owner, or destroy same under Owner's supervision. At Owner's request, Licensee may destroy same and supply Owner with a notarized affidavit of such fact. Upon expiration or other termination of this agreement (except for termination of this agreement by Owner because of Licensee's breach or default under this agreement) Licensee shall have the right to sell, for a period of six months only, any inventory of musical product previously manufactured. However, within fifteen (15) days from such termination or other expiration, Licensee must furnish to Owner a written list of such inventory which also shows the factory costs. Such sales shall be subject to royalty payments by Licensee under the terms of this agreement. However, at any time after the expiration or other termination of this agreement, Owner shall have the right to purchase from Licensee at Licensee's factory cost, all or part of the inventory not sold by Licensee. Such sales shall not be subject to the royalty payments under this agreement.

22. For the purposes of this agreement, the term "musical product" shall mean any disk record of any material and revolving at any speed, any other device of any type, character or description for the reproduction of sound, manufactured or sold primarily for home entertainment, whether embodying sound alone or sound synchronized with visual images (e.g. "sight and sound" devices). It shall also include any printing of sheet music or written publications.

23. Owner represents and warrants that it possesses full right, power and authority to enter into this agreement. Owner will not grant or attempt to grant to any other person, firm or corporation in the Licensed Territory, rights of any kind in any of the aforementioned master recordings. Owner also warrants that there are no liens or encumbrances against any of the recordings which are the subject hereof.

24. The covenants, representations and warranties hereunder are subject to applicable laws and treaties.

25. This agreement shall be deemed made in and shall be construed in accordance with the laws of the State of _____. If any part of this agreement shall be invalid or unenforceable, it shall not affect the validity of the balance of this agreement.

26. **Governing Law**: This Agreement shall be governed by the laws and in the courts of the State of _____ and by the laws of the United States, excluding their conflicts of law principles. Any dispute or legal proceeding regarding the Agreement shall take place in the county of _____, in the State of _____.

Signature below will constitute this as a binding agreement between us.

Dated: _____

Agreed to and Accepted:

_____   _____

Exhibit A – Product Details

Product Name	Product Description	Product Id
_____	_____	_____
_____	_____	_____
_____	_____	_____
_____	_____	_____
_____	_____	_____
_____	_____	_____
_____	_____	_____
_____	_____	_____
_____	_____	_____
_____	_____	_____
_____	_____	_____
_____	_____	_____
_____	_____	_____
_____	_____	_____
_____	_____	_____
_____	_____	_____
_____	_____	_____
_____	_____	_____
_____	_____	_____
_____	_____	_____
_____	_____	_____
_____	_____	_____
_____	_____	_____

YOUR PARTNER IN PROMOTION—THE SPONSOR

We've looked at co-promotion of the products and the licensing of certain products to third parties all in the quest for wider markets but have overlooked an indie label or manager's best friend—the sponsor.

The right sponsor can bring a lot to the table and help keep promotional costs, particularly for events, way down. For example, beer companies and their ad agencies are always looking at new ways to brand a stage. If a band has any following at all, it is likely that a local beer distributor will help out with a huge stage banner. Most regional beer distributors have huge plotter-like printers that can spit out one-off banners easily. In exchange for the free banners (and sometimes even a complete bus wrap), the beer distributor gets logo placement at the best possible place— center stage right behind the artist.

When you are dealing with film or video, the picture can get even rosier. Sponsors have been known to shell out cash in addition to service trades if they can get product placement in video or film. The reason that video or film can demand a higher rate of participation from the sponsor is this form of branding is indelible. When a music video is produced with the sponsor logo branding the video, it is on the video forever. If it is a good video or popular film, the promotional value of this placement for the sponsor could span decades instead of during an event or short-term promotion.

Let's take a look at a sponsorship agreement for an event/tour and see what both the artist, their management, and the sponsor are responsible for.

SPONSORSHIP AGREEMENT

The following will serve as the agreement between _____(Sponsor)_____ (hereinafter referred to as the "Sponsor") and _____(Artist's Management/Promoter)_____(hereinafter referred to as the "Manager") for the services of _____(Artist/Event)_____ (hereinafter referred to as the "Artist/Event") in connection with the Sponsor's products and services (all collectively hereinafter referred to as the "Products").

1.   Sponsor shall be the exclusive sponsor of the Artist/Event tentatively scheduled for ____(Event date or Tour dates)_____. Without limiting the generality of the foregoing, no other party (e.g. a local radio station or product manufacturer) may be listed or mentioned as a sponsor or presenter of the Event/Artist.

2.   As full compensation for the rights and services granted herein, Sponsor shall pay Manager the sum of XXXXX ($xxxxxx.xx) DOLLARS, payable in three (3) equal installments on the following dates:

       June 1, 20__ - $XXXXX.XX

       September 1, 20__ - $XXXXX.XX

       December 1, 20__ - $XXXXX.XX

3.   In connection with said Artist/Event, Sponsor shall receive XXXXXXXX (XX) tickets at no cost for each performance. Such tickets shall be for favorable seats in the highest price range and locations. In addition, Sponsor shall have the right to purchase, at the ticket's face value price, up to ten percent (10%) of concert tickets at each venue, said tickets to be for favorable seats in the highest price range and to be made available at the earliest date(s) possible.

4.   (a)   An official logo and identification phraseology or catch phrase shall be developed for the Artist/Event by manager which shall be subject to the approval of the Sponsor and which shall refer to Sponsor (in first position), Artist/Event (e.g. Sponsor presents Artist/Event). Such logo and/or identification phraseology, where applicable, shall be prominently included in all promotional and advertising references which relate to the Artist/Event and disseminated throughout any media (e.g. print, radio, television and point of sale) by promoter or company announcing the Artist/Event. Nothing herein contained shall constitute an obligation on Sponsor's part to advertise or promote the Artist/Event, it being understood by the parties hereto that the Sponsor may do so at its option or may refrain therefrom.

       (b)   Any uses of the official logo and/or identification phraseology or catch phrase, other than specifically provided for in this Agreement, shall require the prior written permission of both Sponsor and Manager.

5.   (a)   Sponsor's sponsorship of the Artist/Attraction shall be prominently featured and/or displayed in connection with the Artist/Event and all aspects thereof, including but not limited to, references on tickets, passes, handbills,inflatables (where applicable), indoor and outdoor venue signage (where applicable), venue marquee, stationery (if any), press releases, the stage and curtain (where applicable) and a sponsor reference on the front cover of any Official Programs. The form of such sponsorship references shall be subject to the mutual approval of the Sponsor and Manager. Sponsor shall be responsible for providing

banners with its name and/or logo of Sponsor's products and/or references to its sponsorship of the Artist/Event, provided such banners contain references to the Sponsor/Products (which banners Manager shall cause to be prominently displayed in the venue(s)), graphic layouts, vehicles signage (but only if Sponsor requests same) and any other materials deemed necessary or desirable by both Sponsor and Manager. A Sponsor's sponsorship reference(s) shall appear on the backside of all T-shirts and on all other clothing items sold (the manner and location of such sponsorship reference on such other clothing to be determined by Manager and approved by Sponsor), which are offered for sale to the public; provided, however, if Manager feels it advisable, up to twenty-five percent (25%) of such other clothing items offered for sale to the public need not include such sponsorship references. Sponsors' sponsorship reference on T-shirts and other clothing shall be at least one inch in diameter and comparable to the size of any reference to venue or promoter references, and Manager will use his/her best efforts to satisfy Sponsor's reasonable requirements with respect to such sponsorship references. All such Sponsor's sponsorship references shall refer to the promoter or venue in a manner mutually agreeable to Manager and Sponsor. The official logo and/or identification phraseology or catch phrase shall be included in the posters offered for sale by or under the auspices of the Manager or Artist/Event or their perspective agents or licensees.

(b)   Sponsor's products will be the only such products provided in the backstage area and none of the products of Sponsor's competitors shall be publicly consumed by Artist or his/her employees at the venue or otherwise during the term hereof.

6.   Manager shall use his/her best efforts to provide Sponsor with exclusive venue signage and to permit Sponsor to sell and/or distribute its Products at all venues; subject, however, to each venue's rules, regulations, and prior contractual obligations.

7.   Manager shall hold a press conference regarding the Artist/Event on or about _____(date)_____, and, unless Sponsor otherwise agrees, the only reference to Sponsor shall be Sponsor's sponsorship of the Artist/Event.

8.   Sponsor shall have the right to offer a single poster, T-shirts and other items as premium merchandise to the public featuring the identification of one or more of the Sponsor's Products and Artist/Event's name and/or likeness; provided such items shall be subject to Manager's prior approval as to quality, design, appropriateness and consumer value. Sponsor recognizes that Manager and Artist/Event shall be exploiting merchandising rights in connection with Artist/Event and that the Sponsor's premium items shall in some manner differ in design from those offered in connection with the Manager's exploitation of its merchandise rights so as to minimize direct competition between Sponsor's and Manager's respective items being exploited. The poster and other items shall be offered on a free or self-liquidating basis.

9.   Sponsor shall use its best efforts to promote to the public Manager's premium merchandise during the term of this Agreement, provided such material is acceptable to the Sponsor with respect to quality, appropriateness, design and consumer value. Sponsor agrees to use its best efforts to assist Manager to develop merchandise items that meet Sponsor's reasonable criteria as provided herein. Manager shall indemnify Sponsor for any liability in connection with its premium merchandise offer. Sponsor shall likewise indemnify Manager and Artist/Event for any liability from Sponsor's premium merchandise offer, exclusive of product liability relating to the materials provided by Manager.

10.   Artist/Event grants to the Sponsor the right to use the Artist/Event's name and likeness for advertising and promotional materials during the term of this Agreement in connection with the Sponsor's Products on the following terms and conditions:

(a)   Manager or Manager's authorized representative shall be available and shall cooperate in pre-production consultation. Manager shall provide Sponsor with five (5) consecutive full days of the services of Manager and/or Manager's representative(s), tentatively scheduled for the first week in ____(month)____, to produce and record for such advertising and promotional materials. All such work days shall otherwise be at mutually agreeable times.

(b)   From the results of the services rendered pursuant to subparagraph (a) above, the Sponsor may produce two (2) television commercials with two (2) local television tag formats, two (2) local radio tag formats, two (2) print ad designs, two (2) outdoor billboard ad designs and one (1) point of sale design, all for use from January 1, 20__ through December 31, 20__ to promote Sponsor's products separately and/or in connection with the Artist/Event. Print   ads, outdoor billboards and the point of sale pieces can be appropriately modified as to size and other minor modifications, provided such modifications do not change the basic concept.

(c)   The commercial materials produced hereunder may be used throughout the United States, Canada and Mexico during the term of this Agreement.

(d)   Artist/Event shall not endorse nor render any promotion, publicly or advertising services for any product or service retailer anywhere in the territories mentioned in paragraph 10 (c) above nor grant licenses for the name and/or likeness in connection therewith.

11.   The term of this Agreement shall commence with the execution hereof by Sponsor, Manager and/or Artist/Event and shall continue until __(date)__, 20__.

12.   Sponsor shall be given the right of first negotiation and first refusal with respect to the sponsorship, if any, of any television specials or comparable television appearances whether on free, pay or cable television, prominently featuring Artist/Event, which is substantially filmed, taped and/or produced during the term of this Agreement, provided that this right of first negotiation and refusal shall not apply to materials substantially produced, taped and/or filmed prior the effective date of this Agreement.

13.   All trademarks, photos, transparencies and similar production materials produced hereunder shall be the exclusive property of the Manager and shall be returned promptly after the expiration of this Agreement, provided that any underlying music and lyrics provided by Sponsor shall be owned by the Sponsor. Further, following the expiration or termination of this Agreement, no further use whatsoever may be made of official logo by Sponsor, Manager and/or Artist/Event, but the official logo may be used by Manager and Artist/Event without a reference to Sponsor or Sponsor's Product(s).

14.   Manager and Artist/Event shall secure and maintain throughout the term of this Agreement all insurance customarily secured for tours/events of the stature and size, subject to the mutual approval as to the type of insurance and the amount of coverage, which policies may, at the Sponsor's option, name Sponsor as an additional named insured. If Sponsor is so named, Sponsor will bear the proportionate cost of any and all premiums paid on such insurance.

15.   If Manager is prevented from fully performing the terms and conditions of this Agreement due to a Force Majeure as customarily defined in the entertainment industry, Manager and/or Sponsor may suspend and/or terminate this Agreement in accordance with standard

industry provisions for such occurrences, provided in no event shall Manager be obligated to return any sums advanced, loaned or paid hereunder. The parties hereto will attempt in good faith to negotiate a more detailed Force Majeure clause as provided below.

16.   The Sponsor, Manager, and Artist/Event agree that the terms and conditions of this Agreement are confidential and cannot be disclosed to any third party except as expressly provided herein.

17.   Sponsor shall have no liability whatsoever with respect to any commissions due agents of Manager and/or Artist/Event in connection with the securing of this Agreement, all of which obligations shall be contractor's sole liability, and Sponsor shall likewise be solely responsible for any commissions due its agents.

18.   Sponsor shall have the right to hold receptions and other social affairs and events in association with the Artist/Event for the purpose of entertaining clients, retailers, contest winners, etc. Artist/Event shall have the obligation to participate in these receptions.

19.   Artist/Event, Manager and Sponsor warrant and represent they have the right and authority to enter into this Agreement and their performance hereunder shall not conflict with the rights granted any other party. Manager and Artist/Event agree to be jointly and severally liable for the performance of their obligations under this Agreement.

20.   This Agreement is construed and guided in accordance with the laws of the State of _____ and, in the event of any litigation between the parties hereto, __(state)__ laws shall govern and the location of any litigation or arbitration shall be under the jurisdiction of the State of _____.

21.   Should any portion of this Agreement be found to be invalid or unenforceable, it shall not effect the remainder of this Agreement.

22.   This Agreement is intended to be fully binding on the parties hereunder provided this Agreement shall not become effective until formally approved by Artist/Event which approval must occur within seven (7) business days from the date hereto and executed by all other parties listed. It is contemplated that this Agreement between the parties containing additional terms and conditions customarily contained in agreements of this type (e.g. rights to secure life insurance, indemnities, conduct clauses, protection of trademark, reasonable notice and cure provisions, where appropriate, etc.), all of which shall be negotiated in good faith. Provided, however, that until such more detailed agreement is executed, this Agreement shall remain in full force and effect after the approval of the Artist/Event.

In consideration of the terms and obligations of this Agreement, the parties hereto set their hands.

By   _____   By   _____
       Manager   **Sponsor**

By   _____
       Artist/Event

Page 4 of 4

142

MOVING THE GOODS—A LOOK AT PRODUCT CONSIGNMENT

When getting your independently produced product to market, the first place an indie band or manager can start marketing is by leaving the product on consignment in local and regional retail outlets. A good regional or national distribution may be outside the scope of the present situation and setting up consignments is a great way to market test the product and its placement.

There is an old adage in the real estate business that the three most important things are "location, location and location." It is no different in retail. Any store only has so much desirable shelf space and the competition is hot and heavy for good placement in the store. Keep in mind you will be competing with the majors in record stores and it is much harder to place your product in a chain, even locally than in a single store.

Consignment can also be a headache because you wind up doing the duties of the rack jobber—the guy who brings in the new product and arranges it into a sales compelling display. Most stores will take five to ten of your CDs on consignment but may balk at putting a poster or standup display in the store to promote it. It never hurts to ask, but you might be competing with a full-scale color cardboard standup of the major label's most popular artist. Don't forget to give each consignment outlet a free copy of the product and ask them to place it over the in-house music or the listening kiosk.

SALE OF GOODS ON CONSIGNMENT AGREEMENT

This Sale of Goods on Consignment Agreement ("Agreement") is made and effective this [Date], by and between [Consignor] ("Consignor") and [Consignee] ("Consignee").

NOW, THEREFORE, it is agreed:

1. Consignment of Goods.
Consignor shall ship to Consignee, on consignment, the following described goods (the "Goods"): [Goods]. Consignor shall be responsible for the cost of shipping to Consignee. Consignee shall, upon delivery F.O.B. [Destination] receive the Goods and shall store them carefully and properly in Consignee's warehouse to protect them from loss, damage, or deterioration. Consignee shall designate the Goods as the property of Consignor by a conspicuous notice at in Consignee's warehouse, and shall perform all acts required by law to protect the rights of Consignee to the Goods. Consignee, from and after the time it receives the Goods, shall pay all expenses incident thereto, including all expenses of carting, handling, storage, selling, and delivering to customers. Consignee shall at all times observe Consignor's sales rules and procedures with respect to the Goods.

2. Title to Goods.
The Goods shall remain Consignor's property until sold to Consignee's customers, and title to the proceeds of the sales of the Goods shall vest in and belong to Consignor and be held in trust for Consignor's benefit until accounted for and remitted to Consignor.

3. Loss or Damage to Goods.
Consignee shall be responsible to and shall reimburse Consignor for all loss and expense to Consignor resulting from damage to or destruction of the Goods, or from levy or attachment of any court process or lien thereon while in Consignee's possession, and until such time as the title passes from Consignor by reason of the sale thereof and the proceeds of sale have been accounted for and remitted to Consignor. Consignee shall maintain an insurance policy or policies on the Goods in Consignee's possession, protecting against loss from fire and other insurable perils, in an amount satisfactory to Consignor and naming Consignor as insured and loss payee.

4. Report of Sales and Payment.
Not later than the [Day of the Month] of each month Consignee shall make a written report to Consignor listing sales of the Goods made by Consignee during the previous calendar month. Consignee shall remit to Consignor for the Goods so sold an amount equal to: [Formula or Dollar Amount Paid to Consignor]. Consignee shall make such payments to Consignor within [Number of Days to Pay] after the date of each report. If payment is made on or before the fifth (5th) day of the month following the calendar month that the Goods were sold, [Prompt Payment Discount] may be deducted from such remittance as a cash discount. After receiving each report of sales, Consignor shall mail an invoice to Consignee covering the sales shown in such timely report, bearing a date not later than the last day of the same month. Amounts otherwise due shall be paid within fifteen (15) days of invoice.

5. Records.
Consignee shall keep a true record of all Goods in its possession under consignment and shall give the representatives of Consignor access to such record on demand and shall permit such representatives, at reasonable times, to make an inventory of the Goods in Consignee's possession. The consigned Goods shall include the Goods in transit as well as the Goods in Consignee's warehouse.

6. Term and Termination.
The term of this Agreement shall begin [Start Date] and shall remain in force and shall continue thereafter until either party gives to the other party at least [Number of Days Notice] prior written

notice of its intention to terminate, during which time Consignee shall continue to sell the Goods in its possession in accordance with the Agreement. Notwithstanding the foregoing, Consignor may terminate this Agreement without prior notice in the event that Consignee defaults in any material term of this Agreement which default is not cured within ten (10) days' notice from Consignor, and in such event Consignor may remove all Goods from Consignee's premises. Upon Consignor's termination of this Agreement, Consignee shall return all consigned Goods to Consignor F.O.B. at Consignor's facility at [Address of Consignor's Facility], and shall promptly pay to Consignor for all Goods not accounted for by Consignee, at Consignor's wholesale list prices and without any commission, discount, or compensation to Consignee. Upon termination of this Agreement by Consignee, Consignor shall send Consignee an invoice for all Goods in Consignee's possession at prices specified in the preceding sentence, and such invoice shall be paid by Consignee on or before the fifteenth (15th) day of the month following the date of termination.

7. No Authority to Act for Consignor.
Consignee shall conduct the entire business of selling the Goods in Consignee's name and at Consignee's cost and expense. Nothing in this Agreement shall authorize or empower Consignee to assume or create any obligation or responsibility whatsoever, expressed or implied, on behalf or in the name of Consignor, or to bind Consignor in any manner, or make any representation, warranty, or commitment on behalf of Consignor, this Agreement being limited solely to the consignment of the merchandise herein specified.

8. Indemnity.
Consignee shall indemnify Consignor against any loss, damage, suit, liability or claim (including reasonable attorney's fees and costs) caused by acts of Consignee not authorized by this Agreement or by any willful or negligent act of Consignee.

9. Financing Statement.
Consignee shall sign and deliver to Consignor such financing statements, continuation statements and other documents reflecting Consignor's ownership of the Goods, in a form satisfactory to Consignor, as Consignor may from time to time reasonably request. Consignor may, at its sole expense, file any such financing statement or continuation statement. The parties intend that title to the Goods remain in Consignor as provided in this Agreement, and that this Agreement be a consignment in all respects.

10. Benefit.
This Agreement shall be binding upon and inure to the benefit of the parties hereto, and their respective successors and assigns, but it shall not be assigned by Consignee without the prior written consent of Consignor.

11. Taxes.
Consignor shall be responsible for the payment of all income taxes accruing to Consignor for revenue received from the sale of the Goods. Consignee shall be responsible for any sales, use or excise taxes resulting from the sale of the Goods to Consignee's customers. Consignee shall also be responsible for all income taxes accruing to Consignee on the commission revenue from its sale of the Goods and for personal property taxes and other charges or levies imposed on the Goods while in Consignee's possession.

12. Notices.
Any notice required by this Agreement or given in connection with it, shall be in writing and shall be given to the appropriate party by personal delivery or by certified mail, postage prepaid, or recognized overnight delivery services.

If to Consignor:

__Consignor's Name/Address___

If to Consignee:

__Consignee's Name/Address___

13. Final Agreement.
This Agreement terminates and supersedes all prior understandings or agreements on the subject matter hereof. This Agreement may be modified only by a further writing that is duly executed by both parties.

14. Governing Law.
This Agreement shall be construed and enforced in accordance with the laws of the state of [State of Governing Law].

15. Headings.
Headings used in this Agreement are provided for convenience only and shall not be used to construe meaning or intent.

IN WITNESS WHEREOF, the parties have executed this Agreement.

_____
Consignor

_____
Consignee

CHAPTER 11

Working with Publicists

Lee Roy Parnell, Courtesy of The Music Office

A key player in the entertainment business is the publicist. Going from total obscurity to becoming a household name is not an easy task. The manager (or the artist/band if there is no manager) will retain the publicist to get press and media exposure. To accomplish this, the publicist needs to exercise rights that are in some way similar to those of the manager. The publicist needs to be fed good information from the manager or group and has to have the power to act in the artist's name in all things regarding publicity and public image. Just as you would send an offer for a performance to your agent or a product endorsement to your manager, you will direct all press and media inquiries to your publicist. Also, similarly to the management agreement, you will probably be required to execute a power of attorney to the publicist to act in your name regarding matters of promotion in the press and media. Let's dive into an arrangement between a publicist and artist.

ARTIST PUBLICITY AGREEMENT

1.   This Agreement shall be effective as of the date set forth herein.

2.   This Agreement is entered into, guided by and governed by the laws of the State of
_____. Should any portion of this Agreement be found to be invalid or unenforceable, it shall
not affect the balance of this Agreement.

3.   The parties to this Agreement shall be:

    (a)   _____ (hereinafter referred to and the
              "Artist") and;

    (b)   _____ (hereinafter referred to as the
              "Publicist".

4.   The parties have discussed the matter of how long this Agreement shall be in effect.
They have discussed the advantages and disadvantages of a short-term, medium-term, and/or
long-term Agreement. The parties agree that duration of this Agreement shall be THREE YEARS.

5.   Publicist agrees to perform on behalf of Artist the services customarily rendered on behalf
of artists.   Publicist agrees to perform the following services when requested to do so by the
Artist:

    (a)   Advise and counsel in any matters pertaining to publicity, public relations and
             advertising in all fields of entertainment.

    (b)   Advise and counsel in the selection of literary, artistic and musical material as far
             as publicity value is concerned.

    (c)   Advise and counsel with relation to the proper format for presentation of Artist's
             artistic talents and in the determination of proper style, mood, setting, business
             and characterization in keeping with the Artist's talents as far as publicity value is
             concerned.

    (d)   Advise and counsel and direct in the selection of the artist's talent to assist,
             accompany or embellish Artist's artistic presentation as far as publicity value is
             concerned.

    (e)   Advise and counsel with regard to general parties in the entertainment and
             amusements industries as far as publicity is concerned.

    (f)   Advise and counsel the selection of publicity programs.

    (g)   Unpaid Television and Radio interviews (unless forbidden by AFTRA),
             newspaper and magazine interviews and pictures shall be sought.

    (h)   Mail publicity releases to the trade press, fan magazines, newspaper columnists,
             and radio and television interview shows, etc.

    (i)   Co-operate with public relations personnel if Artist, his employer(s) and/or his
             management.

6.   (a)   Publicist hereby informs Artist that stories and items may contain incorrect
             information about the Artist; such information may result from Publicist being
             misinformed or because the publication in which the story or item appears made

an intentional error and/or omission, or for other reasons. Publicist hereby informs Artist that Artist may suffer embarrassment and annoyance because of correct and incorrect publicity. Artist declares that he understands that he may suffer mental anguish and monetary loss because of publicity. Artist hereby authorizes Publicist to release any and all information about him.

> (i)   Artist agrees that Publicist does not need to clear copy with the Artist.

> (ii)   Publicist will keep a copy of all releases and articles the Publicist can amass in a file at Publicist's office which the Artist can make use of.

(b)   Artist promises to supply Publicist with many different pictures and copies of resumes at Artist's cost. Pictures shall be 8" x 10". Publicist hereby notifies Artist that Publicist will be handicapped in his work if he does not receive pictures and resumes in the quantity requested.

7.   Artist hereby authorizes and appoints publicist as his agent and attorney-in-fact to:

(a)   Approve and permit all publicity, public relations, endorsements, etc.

(b)   Approve and permit the use of Artist's name, photograph, likeness, voice, sound effects, caricatures, literary, artistic and musical material for the purposes of advertising and publicity and in the promotion and advertising of any and all products, services, etc.

8.   Artist agrees to at all times to devote himself to his career, to do all things necessary and desirable to promote his career and earnings therefrom. Artist agrees to at all times engage proper theatrical agencies to obtain engagements and employment for him.

9.   Artist and Publicist agree that Publicist is not an employment agent, theatrical agent, or licensed artist's manager or personal manager. The parties agree that Publicist is not obligated to attempt to secure employment or engagements for Artist. The parties agree that Publicist has not promised to procure employment or engagements for Artist.

10.   This Agreement shall not be construed to create a partnership or joint venture between Artist and Publicist. It is an Agreement between independent contractors. Artist desires to benefit from that which the Publicist can do. Artist desires to compensate Publicist. Artist does not desire to obligate himself to pay Publicist large amounts of dollars per hour, day, week, month, year, or any other period. Artist does desire a relationship to exist between the compensation to Publicist and Artist's ability to pay. Artist understands the difficulties in finding a 100% accurate manner in measuring the value of Publicist's services. Occasionally in the business an Artist pays to a person performing the services Publicist shall perform on behalf of Artist, a percentage of the income of the Artist. Both parties understand that Artist may have the benefit of receiving work from Publicist which will far exceed the amount of money that Publicist will receive. Both parties understand that in the event Artist's income shall be in the thousands, or tens of thousands or hundreds of thousands of dollars per month, year or other time period, Publicist's income from Artist will exceed the amount Artist would have to pay to salaried Contractors if Artist at that time would employ salaried Contractors to perform Publicist's functions.

11.   The parties understand that Publicist's position is that of an independent contractor. Publicist may appoint or engage other persons, firms or corporations to perform any and all services (both routine and non-routine) that this Agreement states Publicist shall perform. Publicist's services are not exclusive - Publicist is now and shall continue to perform somewhat

similar services for other artists; also Publicist is now interested in several businesses and Publicist shall continue to devote time to those businesses and to new businesses.

12.   The parties understand that there may be times when Artist may be unhappy with Publicist, or Publicist may be unhappy with Artist, or both may be unhappy with each other. The parties realize that there may be times when Artist will desire that Publicist perform certain work and that Publicist will not perform the desired work or may not even commence to perform the desired work. There may be times when Publicist will desire that Artist will perform certain work which Artist believes will aid Artist's career, such as appearing at interviews, speaking engagements, photographic sessions and the like.

THEREFORE, the parties agree, that Publicist shall be required to perform and render reasonable services as and when reasonably requested by Artist. It is agreed that Publicist shall not be deemed in default hereunder unless and until Artist shall first deliver to Publicist by written notice, registered mail describing the exact nature of the service which Artist requires of Publicist and then only in the event that Publicist shall therefore fail for a period of fifteen (15) consecutive days to commence the rendition for the particular service required.

The parties agree that Artist shall not be in default hereunder unless and until Publicist has notified Artist by written, registered mail about the work that Publicist considers Artist is duty bound to perform in accordance with the provisions of this Agreement entered into by Publicist under the authority of this Agreement.

13.   (a)   Publicist shall be reimbursed for expenses if, and only if, Publicist gives to Artist receipts for such expenses within two (2) weeks after incurring or paying them, whichever is later.

        (b)   Publicist shall not be required to travel or to meet Artist at any particular place. The parties agree that under the terms of this Agreement they may agree at a future time that Publicist may travel and that arrangements will then be made for costs and expenses of such travel. These arrangements may be to the effect that Artist will pay for any or all of Publicist's travel expenses. Unless otherwise agreed to in the future, Artist shall pay Publicist's travel expenses incurred but Publicist will have Artist grant his permission and approval of such expenses in advance of incurring them.

14.   As a partial fee for Publicist's services, Artist agrees to pay Publicist, as and when received by Artist, and during the term hereof, a sum equal to _____ per ___(week/month)_____.

15.   In the event Publicist has not received payment from Artist for services rendered hereunder for two billing periods (one month), Publicist shall have the option and right to cease and desist from working in the client's behalf and to take action against him for nonpayment.

16.   This Agreement constitutes the sole and complete agreement between the Parties hereto, superseding and invalidating all previous agreements, both written and oral.

17.   Should any portion of this Agreement be found to be invalid or unenforceable, it shall not affect the validity of the balance of this Agreement.

18.   Artist and Publicist each warrant to the other that each is able to enter into and abide by the terms of this agreement, that there are no existing agreements which would interfere with the pursuit of each of the tasks each agrees to perform.

Page 3 of 4

THE PARTIES HEREBY agree to and will abide by the terms of this Agreement by so setting their names below.

_____   _____
ARTIST   **PUBLICIST**

By: _____   **By:** _____

THE STATE OF _____   )
)
COUNTY OF _____   )

    I, _____, a Notary Public, do hereby certify that on this _____ day of _____,20___, personally appeared before me _____, known to me to be the person whose name is subscriber to the foregoing instrument, and swore and acknowledged to me that he executed the same for the purpose and in the capacity therein expressed, and that the statements contained therein are true and correct.

_____

NOTARY PUBLIC, STATE OF _____

_____
Name, Typed or Printed

My Commission Expires: _____

CHAPTER 12

Working with or as Photographers and Videographers

Mike McDonald and Becka Brammlet, Courtesy of The Music Office

I'm probably going to make enemies out of a number of photographers out there, but I have to shoot from the hip regarding this aspect of the music business. Let me start with a quick anecdote.

In the mid '80s, I was working with an artist on an independent label. The project was reasonably well funded—so much as to hire enough radio plugging muscle to chart nationally.

A photographer was hired to take photos for the album cover. The photographer was good and demanded a large daily rate. The shoot went off and that was what we thought was the last we would see of the shutter bug.

About six months later, about one week into the CD release nationally, we get a phone call from the photographer claiming infringement on the copyright of his photos that were printed on the CD. I asked him what he assumed we were going to do with the photos taken at a "CD cover shoot." He said that was immaterial and he never signed a release nor licensed the photos to us. He threatened to sue, knowing the project backer had deep pockets and might be amendable to extortion seeing how the product was already in stores.

I had to sit back a minute and take a deep breath. I called the photographer back and said there must be some misunderstanding. Reviewing our records we had to inform the photographer that not only the artist's music was under our exclusive control but her image also. Further we could not find any document licensing the photographer giving him permission to utilize for commercial exploitation the image of the artist we owned exclusively.

I told him we viewed his work on a work-for-hire basis and if he didn't like it, suck eggs. Sue us if you must. We'll see you in court. We never heard from him again.

Consequently, I never retain the services of a photographer except under a work-for-hire arrangement. All the images he takes are our property exclusively. I have gone even further by demanding that the film be processed by us or if shot digitally we get the raw images at the time and place of the shoot. Photographers hate me. The following agreement is short, simple and to the point.

PHOTOGRAPHER CONTRACT

THIS AGREEMENT, made this _____ day of _____, 20__, is for the services described below between the undersigned PHOTOGRAPHER and the undersigned CLIENT.

The undersigned parties hereby agree that all rights, copyrights, titles and interest in any photographs taken by PHOTOGRAPHER on behalf of CLIENT belong solely and exclusively to the CLIENT and are free from any claims whatsoever by the PHOTOGRAPHER.

CLIENT promises to pay PHOTOGRAPHER the sum of _____ ($ _____). This is a one-time payment for PHOTOGRAPHER'S services and will be considered complete and sole compensation for services rendered.

GOVERNING LAW: This Agreement shall be governed by the laws and in the courts of the State of _____ and by the laws of the United States, excluding their conflicts of law principles. Any dispute or legal proceeding regarding the Agreement shall take place in the county of _____, in the State of _____.

Your signature below will constitute this as a binding agreement between us.

DATED: _____

AGREED TO AND ACCEPTED

For PHOTOGRAPHER _____   For CLIENT _____

Signature _____   Signature _____

TALENT/MODEL RELEASE

From the other side of the lens, the form shown on page 156 should be in every photographer's kit: a photographic model release form. I am so glad that the photographer mentioned in the story above didn't have one.

Talent/Model Release

Wang Dang Video Productions
123 Elm Parkway
Elsewhere, PA 87654

In consideration of the sum of $1.00 and any other good and valuable considerations, receipt of which is hereby acknowledged, I, being of legal age, hereby give [Production Company Name], their licensees, successors, legal representatives, and assigns the absolute and irrevocable right and permission to use my name and to use, reproduce, edit, exhibit, project, display, copyright, publish and/or resell photography images and/or moving pictures and/or videotaped images of me with or without my voice, or in which I may be included in whole or in part, photographed, taped, videotaped, and/or recorded on [date] and thereafter, and to circulate the same in all forms and media for art, advertising, trade, competition of every description and/or any other lawful purpose whatsoever. I also consent to the use of any printed matter in conjunction therewith.

I hereby waive any right that I may have to inspect and/or approve the finished product or products or the editorial, advertising, or printed copy or soundtrack that may be used in connection therewith and any right that I may have to control the use to which said product, products, copy and/or soundtrack may be applied.

I hereby release, discharge and agree to save [Production Company Name], their licensees, successors, legal representatives and assigns from any liability by virtue of any blurring, distortion, alteration, optical illusion or use in composite form whether intentional or otherwise that may occur or be produced in the making, processing, duplication, projecting or displaying of said picture or images, and from liability for violation of any personal or proprietary right that I may have in conjunction with said pictures or images and with the use thereof.

AGREED AND ACCEPTED this ___ of _____, 20__.

_____
Model or Parent/Legal Guardian if model is a minor.

Street Address: _____
City: _____, State: _____, Zip: _____
Phone: _____ Social Security #: _____

VIDEOGRAPHY AND FILM CONCERNS

When it comes to getting the act's image before the public, you can't beat television or film exposure. You can reach an audience far larger than you would in any venue if the right exposure comes your way. A common place to start in many cities is to get a slot on a public access show. Here is the simple one-page release that the local TV station requires talent to sign. The release is pretty short and to the point. If I was being a bit pickier I might insert a clause that gives a term to the video release—say five years. As the contract stipulates that it is not for commercial gain, it is probably a moot point.

Public Access Video Release

I, _____, hereby grant _____ and its agents the right to video/audio tape my likeness/voice/performance and/or the likeness/voice/performance of _____ (name of group), in connection with the production and distribution of the video/audio tape presentation named below, and that said video/audio tape may be cablecast, broadcast or otherwise transmitted by _____ its successors or assigns. I agree that you may copyright said video/audio tape.

I further agree that my name(s) likeness/voice(s) and biographical material may be used in connection with publicity about the production named below.

I understand that the recorded material will not be used for commercial gain, but excerpts may be used in compilations or other promotional activities. I release _____ and their agents, successors and assigns from further claims or demands arising from the uses of materials you may record in which I/we appear or can be heard.

Production: _____

Date: _____

Signature: _____

Address: _____
_____
_____

Phone: _____

An actor release for a small no-budget indie film or documentary is shown on page 159. The actor is paid with that old die-hard of broke productions—a piece of the backend action or net profits. It is what any actor would regard as a "spec" deal (meaning don't "spec" to be paid). The author of this contract might have included the generous "One Dollar" clause, but even that may have been outside the budget.

If you are working as a videographer, filmmaker or even a cameraman, it is a good idea to have a bundle of video releases on hand so you can tie up your legal loose ends at the time it is easiest to do so—at the shoot.

Different production companies look at it in different ways, but my general rule of thumb is that you can't get too many releases. I recently finished a short documentary. A talent release, location release, and permission to use a manufacturer's product image all had to be acquired.

When I produce a live concert video, I have an audience sign-in sheet and release that each audience member has to sign to enter the theater or venue. If they balk, I let them know that they can still hear the concert—from the parking lot.

LOCATION RELEASE

We've covered the actors and on-camera talent, but it is also necessary to get a release from the location where you are shooting the video, especially if it is a commercial enterprise. The release we recently used for the documentary is shown on pages 160–162.

ACTOR AGREEMENT

This agreement is entered into by and between _____ (the "Actor") and _____ (the "Production Company"). In the event of the Actor's death or total incapacity, "Actor" means the Actor's heirs, devisees, beneficiaries, trusts, assignees or other successors-in-interest. "Production Company" includes the licensees, assignees, future owners, or other acquirers or successors-in-interest of the Production Company.

The Actor hereby grants to the Production Company and to its licensees, assignees, and other successors-in-interest, all rights of every kind and character, in perpetuity, in and to the Actor's performance, appearance, likeness, name and/or voice (the "Performance") in connection with the motion picture entitled _____ which is based on the concept and outline by _____ (the "Picture").

The Actor hereby authorizes the Production Company to photograph, videotape, film and record (on film, tape, or any other medium), the Performance and audition(s) for the Performance; to edit the same at its discretion and to include it with the performances of others and with sound effects, special effects, digital effects and music; to incorporate the same into the Picture, trailers, posters or other materials or programs related to the Picture; to use and to license others to use such records and photographs in any manner or media whatsoever, including without limitation unrestricted use for purposes of publicity, advertising and sales promotion; and to use my name, likeness, voice, biography or other information concerning me in connection with the Picture and for any other purpose associated with the Picture. The Actor further acknowledges that the Production Company owns all rights to the Picture.

The Production Company shall compensate the Actor for the Performance by payment to Actor of ___% of net profits to the Production Company from all distribution and exploitation of the Picture (including Picture trademarks, service marks, logos, slogans, likenesses, names, voice, or dialog), including royalties, dividends, or payments of any kind arising from theater, television, video, CD, DVD, or Internet distribution and exploitation. Net profits shall be determined in accordance with generally accepted accounting principles. Payment will be made to the Actor on a quarterly basis in perpetuity as the Production Company receives such monies. The Actor is responsible to pay all applicable taxes and other assessments or levies of any kind due on the receipt of income.

Unless otherwise agreed to in writing by the Production Company, the Actor will receive no compensation in the event that the Actor does not complete the Performance.

This Agreement constitutes the entire agreement by and between the Actor and the Production Company and supersedes any and all prior contracts, understandings, negotiations, and agreements with respect to the Production Company and the subject matter hereof, whether oral or written.

Actor Name: _____   Signature: _____

Production Company: _____

Location Release

Dated: As of _____, 20__
[Insert Name]
[Insert Address]
Re: Location Address:

_____

Dear Sir or Madam:

This is to confirm the consent and agreement of _____ ("Licensor"), in consideration
of _____ [Insert any compensation terms or delete line] and
the possibility of publicity that __Production/Show Name_____ ("Company"), its agents,
licensees, assigns, successors, parents, subsidiaries and affiliates, and each of their respective
employees, officers, directors, shareholders, agents and representatives are hereby granted the
right and license to enter and remain upon the premises located at
_____ ("Location"), and to make
use of such premises and related Property, from _____ [Insert date] to _____
[Insert date] (plus any reasonable number of re-shoot days subject to availability of the Location
in connection with print, graphic, audio and/or visual or other content, projects, campaigns or
programs, and derivative works thereof [known as "_____"] [Insert Project name]
(the "Project"). Further, Licensor irrevocably grants to The Company the following permissions,
rights and licenses in and to all property, both real and personal, located at such Location
(collectively, the "Property").

In consideration of adequate compensation the receipt of which is acknowledged, Licensor
agrees as follows:

1. **Special Terms and Conditions.** [Insert any special terms, conditions, limitations, etc. (e.g.,
insurance requirement, hours of access, use of utilities, etc.)] [or insert "None"]

2. **Scope.**
   (a) The right and license to photograph, record, depict, represent and otherwise make use
   of the Property. Without limitation, the Property includes any and all names, addresses
   and trademarks connected with the Property and any signs, artwork, sculptures, pictures,
   fixtures and other personal property located thereon, and any logos and verbiage
   contained thereon in connection with, or as part of, the Project, the right to refer to the
   Property by any real or fictitious name, the right to attribute any real or fictitious events
   as having occurred on the Property and the right to reconstruct or recreate the Property or
   any part thereof for use as a set for shooting, photographing, recording and/or filming of
   the Project.
   (b) The right and license to reproduce, publish, distribute, exhibit, sublicense, advertise
   and otherwise exploit any and all productions and materials, in whole or in part, in
   connection with the permissions, rights and licenses hereunder, including, without
   limitation, the Project and the advertising and publicity therefore, and in commercial tie-
   ins and any merchandising or other commercial exploitation of the Project and the allied,

ancillary and subsidiary rights thereto, by any and all methods and manners and in any and all languages, formats and media (including, without limitation, film, television, videocassettes, DVDs, interactive devices and Internet and on-line systems etc.), whether now known or hereafter devised, throughout the world, in perpetuity, without limitation or restriction of any kind and without further payment of any kind.

(c) As between the Licensor and The Company, The Company shall be the sole, exclusive and perpetual owner of all right, title and interest in the Project and any photographs and recordings made hereunder in connection with the Property including, without limitation, the copyright and all renewals and extensions of copyright therein.

3. **Representations/Warranties/Indemnity**. The Licensor represents and warrants that the Licensor has the full right and authority to enter into this "Location Release" and to grant to The Company all of the rights set forth herein and that the consent or permission of no other person or entity is necessary to grant the permissions, rights and licenses contained in this Location Release. The Licensor agrees to indemnify and hold harmless The Company and its parent, and its and their agents, licensees, assigns, successors, subsidiaries and affiliates, and the officers, directors, managers, equity holders, agents and employees of each of them, from and against, any and all losses, costs, liabilities, judgments, damages, claims and expenses (including reasonable outside attorney's fees and costs) of any nature arising from any breach or any alleged breach by the Licensor of any representation, warranty or agreement made by the Licensor in this Location Release

4. **Miscellaneous**. Neither The Company nor its agents, licensees, assigns, successors, parents, subsidiaries and affiliates shall be obligated to photograph scenes or make recordings at or otherwise use the Property, or make any actual use of or reference to any photographs or recordings made at the Property, or otherwise depict or refer to the Property in the Project, or produce, publish, distribute or exploit the Project. The Licensor hereby irrevocably waives and relinquishes any right to seek or obtain, for any reason whatsoever, an injunction, a rescission or termination of this Location Release or any rights hereunder, or any other form of equitable relief against The Company, or otherwise interfere with or impair the development, production, publication, distribution, exhibition, advertising, publicizing or other exploitation of the Project, the Licensor's sole remedy with respect thereto being an action at law for damages (if any).

The Licensor shall have no equitable or legal cause of action against The Company or any third party on the basis that The Company's use of any photographs or recordings made at the Property is, or is claimed to be, defamatory, derogatory, denigrative, untrue, censorable or violative of anyone's rights of privacy or publicity or other personal and/or property rights except insofar as The Company is in material breach of any restrictions specifically set forth in this Location Release (if any). The Licensor acknowledges and agrees that any breach by the Licensor of this Location Release will cause The Company irreparable harm, and therefore, that The Company shall be entitled to injunctive or equitable relief (without obligation to post bond or surety or establish harm) in addition to all other remedies available at law or in equity, in any court of competent jurisdiction.

The Company may freely license, sublicense and assign, in whole or in part, the Location Release or any of the rights hereunder. This is the entire agreement between the parties relating to the matters herein and subsequent to execution cannot be modified without written consent of the parties hereto and shall be exclusively governed by and construed in accordance with the internal laws of the original to:

The Company
234 S. Main St.
Elsewhere, NY 10023

_____
For Company

AGREED AND ACCEPTED to:

_____
Licensor

Page 3 of 3

RELEASE AGREEMENT

If you are hiring an outside contractor for your video, photographic, or film work, the contractor will probably take care of releases—if they are professionals. One of the legal foundations of photographic and video work revolves around the release. The subject in the photo/video has to consent to their image being used—especially for commercial exploitation. The release agreement that follows on page 163 is a general release. I have used it for video shoot sign-in sheets by adding lines for audience members to sign if they wish to participate.

BROADCAST RELEASE

The last release we will visit is the broadcast release. This release has evolved over several programs from public access to commercial stations. It is similar to contracts many television stations and cable providers will require you to sign before submitting videos for airplay. I also used it in conjunction with the video release (above) I get from the artist. The artist has now granted me ownership rights to the program I have produced and consequently permission to broadcast it and enter into contracts like you will find on page 164.

Release Agreement

Whereas, _____ (the "Producer") is engaged in a project (the "Video"), and

Whereas, I, the undersigned, have agreed to appear in the Video, and

Whereas, I understand that my voice, name, and image will be recorded by various mechanical and electrical means of all descriptions (such recordings, any piece thereof, the contents therein and all reproductions thereof, along with the utilization of my name, shall be collectively referred to herein as the "Released Subject Matter").

Therefore, in exchange for $1.00, receipt of which is hereby acknowledged and whose sufficiency as consideration I affirm, I hereby freely and without restraint consent to and give unto the Producer and its agents or assigns or anyone authorized by the Producer, (collectively referred to herein as the "Releasees") the unrestrained right in perpetuity to own, utilize, or alter the Released Subject Matter, in any manner the Releasees may see fit and for any purpose whatsoever, all of the foregoing to be without limitation of any kind. Without limiting the generality of the foregoing, I hereby authorize the Releasees and grant unto them the unrestrained rights to utilize the Released Subject Matter in connection with the Video's advertising, publicity, public displays, and exhibitions. I hereby stipulate that the Released Subject Matter is the property of the Producer to do with as it will.

I hereby waive to the fullest extent that I may lawfully do so, any causes of action in law or equity I may have or may hereafter acquire against the Releasees or any of them for libel, slander, invasion of privacy, copyright or trademark violation, right of publicity, or false light arising out of or in connection with the utilization by the Releasees or another of the Released Subject Matter.

It is my intention that the above mentioned consideration represents the sole compensation that I am entitled to receive in connection with any and all usages of the Released Subject Matter. I expressly stipulate that the Releasees may utilize the Released Subject Matter or not as they choose in their sole discretion without affecting the validity of this Release. This Release shall be governed by _____(state) law.

I hereby certify that I am over the age of eighteen, and that I have read, understood, and agreed to the foregoing.

Signature: _____
Date: _____
Name: _____
Address: _____

BROADCAST RELEASE

THIS AGREEMENT is for the services described below between the undersigned First Party (includes accompanying musicians and/or entertainers as described below, hereinafter referred to as "Artist") and _____ (hereinafter referred to as "Company").

1. Artist consents to the recording and the broadcast of reproduction(s) of the Artist's voice and music as part of _____ (hereinafter referred to as "Program").

2. Artist does hereby acknowledge that the Company is the sole owner of all rights to the Program and the recording thereof, for all purposes. Artist also acknowledges that the Company has the right to broadcast the Program one or more times over any station or cable system. Any materials relating to the production and broadcast of the PROGRAM become property of the Company.

3. Artist understands and agrees to receive the following compensation for appearances on and participation in the Program.

    a. _____

4. Artist's name and likeness may be used in advertising and promotional material for the Program, but not as an endorsement of any product or service.

5. Artist hereby releases and discharges Station _____ from any and all liability in connection with the making, producing, reproducing, processing, exhibiting, distributing, publishing, transmitting by any means or otherwise using the above-mentioned production.

6. All rights to Artist's performance described herein shall remain the sole property of the ARTIST and the rights granted herein are for radio broadcast only. This release does not include any rights to mechanical reproduction of the music (phonorecords, compact discs or any other form of reproduction that may now exist or may come into being).

7. GOVERNING LAW: This AGREEMENT shall be governed by the laws and in the courts of the State of _____ and by the laws of the United States, excluding their conflicts of law principles. Any dispute or legal proceeding regarding the AGREEMENT shall take place in the county of _____, in the State of _____.

Your signature below will constitute this as a binding agreement between us.

DATED: _____

AGREED TO AND ACCEPTED

_____   _____
For Artist   For Company

Part IV

The Future

CHAPTER 13

360° Management Deals

Kristian Fjelstad, Courtesy of The Music Office

THE 360° RECORDING OR MANAGEMENT DEAL

In recent years the major record labels have seen major changes in the landscape of their industry. Not too many years ago, the sales of records was the largest portion of an artist's income. According to *The Economist*, in 2000 almost two-thirds of a musician's earnings were derived from record sales. At the time of this writing (2008) the trend has reversed with artists now seeing almost 70 percent of their income coming from non-record sales sources. The lion's share of this new income is from concert performances and merchandising. The live concert industry is growing; from $1.7 billion in 2000 to $3.1 billion by 2006 and the record companies are viewing this revenue stream with envy. The product the labels are now trying to sell to new artists is the "360° deal." Instead of just negotiating exclusive rights to the artist's recordings, many labels are offering a more "comprehensive" way of developing and controlling an artist's career. In exchange for greater investment and support from the label, the artist gives up the rights to more areas in their career. The labels now want to join the artist as an equity participant in income from many other sources including publishing, booking, endorsements and even management. It smells much like the old Hollywood formula from the 1930s and 1940s where the studio in essence owned the actor. Everything related to the actor's career and even much of their personal life was directed by the studio. Generally speaking, the platform hasn't been around long enough to gauge its success and whether this new cut into an artist's other income can staunch the flow of red ink from the record label's bottom line. Some of the artist and management response to this trend has been less than enthusiastic.

THE LABEL'S POSITION

The labels see themselves as underwriting and promoting these other income streams yet not participating in any of the pay-off. They are taking all the risks in promoting a new act. Who would ever have heard of, much less buy a t-shirt from the Today Tones if the label hadn't spent a fortune promoting the band? The label spends a ton of money only to later bid for the artist's time against agents and management entities that want the group to be out earning—not promoting—record sales. Artists and their management, like any other business people, follow the money. And the weight of the label's enticements has been reduced in the digital age. An up and coming act can see the label as a career one-stop for all their needs and can focus more on being creative. Having a bigger piece of the artist's total income is incentive for the labels to push harder into not only selling recordings, but all the ancillary products that go along with a successful artist. It also brings the label into a longer-term view of their relationship with the artist.

THE ARTIST AND MANAGEMENT POSITION

Australian music lawyer Brett Oaten is not endorsing the concept yet, "Their pitch is 'Our business isn't going so well, so can we have some of your other money please?' I don't believe that is a particularly compelling case." Another point commonly made is whether or not the record labels have the expertise to successfully enter into these areas that they have little or no experience with. Do they know how to fully exploit the rights they have been granted? Agents, and particularly managers, have a personal relationship with their artists and their information and guidance can be invaluable. These are not skills picked up at Harvard Business School, but on the streets and in the trenches of the business.

The label's lack of vision and business inflexibility has brought them to this position of fighting consumer choice and innovation at every turn rather than embracing it. Who is to say that they won't be as inept in management as they have been in responding to emerging technologies? Also, these long-term deals can tie up an artist for their entire career. When tied this closely to a label with this many marketable components in play, the divorce, if even possible, could be quite messy.

Is a label going to follow through with the massive support promised if a band falls out of grace with the public? Are the labels going to continue to pour money at a band who is only selling a few units? What happens to bands that dissolve?

OTHER LABEL METHODS—THE BUYOUT

For years the majors have been gobbling up smaller labels and merging with other large ones. Over the last half century, the number of labels that control over 90 percent of the industry has diminished from hundreds of companies to only four. When a smaller label sells to a larger corporation, the artists in the roster are conveyed in the deal. This is why you will find assignability clauses in all recording and publishing contracts. Possible conflicts of interest could arise if a label were to buy a booking agency and give artists signed to the label preferential treatment.

What is changing is the labels are getting into a larger segment of the industry by buying successful businesses—primarily management and talent agencies although they are growing the merchandising and endorsement portion of their assets to tie in with the 360° deals we looked at earlier.

CHAPTER 14

Digital Rights Management and Binary Branding

David Broza, Courtesy of The Music Office

DRM (DIGITAL RIGHTS MANAGEMENT)

Digital Rights Management has been a subject of much contention over the past few years. Caught asleep at the wheel again, the recording industry was late to the Internet game and found that the model for music distribution was created and being utilized before the industry had a chance to intervene. The music download genie was released from the bottle and the industry, primary behind the marching cadres of the RIAA. (Recording Industry of Association of America), has been battling uphill since to try to reclaim what they view as their birthright to control the distribution of commercial music.

Digital Rights Management is a great idea but it has been so poorly deployed and marketed that many consumers steer clear of Websites and vendors who will only sell heavily protected downloads. The consumer believes that it is their right to purchase a song or CD and to be able to "rip" it onto a CD to play in the car or download it to their iPod or other MP3 player. The recording industry, in a step away from their previous stance, no longer feels you have that right. It is an issue being hotly contested in Congress with the RIAA battling every entertainment consumer group out there.

The actual use of DRM is also a moving target with Congress, the RIAA, and consumer groups fighting over the different flavors of digital delivery. As I write these words, there are workgroups in Congress and the RIAA trying to define what the difference, if any, is between a streamed song and a downloaded file. In technological terms they share much the same template but in general you don't rip a stream so a copy isn't being made. The RIAA's position is that, although unlikely and probably beyond the technical capabilities of the common consumer, the stream could be ripped with a bit of work and that constitutes a digital delivery of the song to the customer. This is sometimes referred to as the labels trying to "double dip" into the consumer's pocket on payments of royalties.

One of the problems the RIAA faces is that historically, performance royalties were not inside their jurisdiction. When a radio station wants to play the latest release from Creed, they have to pay a blanket license to ASCAP, BMI, and SESAC for the right to broadcast the music over the airwaves. The dollar amount of the annual blanket license is tied to the station's income. The labels viewed radio airplay as free promotion and didn't try to get their hands in the pocket of the radio stations that were promoting their artists with airplay. Now the situation has turned 180 degrees and the labels want a piece of the performance pie, even though they never have in the past.

WHERE DO WE GO FROM HERE?

Like it or not, the future is racing toward us and you are going to be a part of it. There are some promising trends in the industry as of this writing that could reshape the way we listen to and purchase music. The most important trend is obviously the Internet. The playing field has been leveled somewhat. The trend is to build your career in-house and avoid partnering with the major labels everywhere you can. A fulfilling career with good earnings can be found without ever knocking on the major's doors. If your college roommate is a computer ninja, it is possible that your Website could be as cool, or cooler than, the site of a major label band.

THE RIAA

The RIAA is generally cast as the villain in the digital rights war. Due to their arriving late to the party, the tried to make up for lost time by using heavy-handed legal maneuvering and lobbying to staunch the flow of their copyrights into the hand of non-paying customers and fans.

No songwriter, musician, or record label wants all music to be downloaded free to anyone that wants it. The "music should be free" crowd is not made up of people who create, produce, or distribute music. It appears to be made up of petty thieves that believe that they have the right to download, use, and even share the intellectual properties of the label or band without paying anything. I wonder if any of these people would like it if they went to work the next morning to find that their boss had a new policy: you still do the work, but we don't pay you for it because, "labor wants to be free."

From where I am sitting, the biggest problem the RIAA faces is not the rampant piracy occurring on the Internet, but that the foundation and model of their industry is outdated and out of touch with all the other players, the musicians, the publishers, and most importantly, the public.

I would like to make a quick note regarding who the RIAA really is. When it was created in the 1950s, the RIAA was primarily a standards group. The RIAA set the standards for audio fidelity on phonorecords and later cassette, film audio protocols, and other technical aspects that grew to be standards.

The RIAA also certifies record sales, so when you see the moniker, "platinum selling album," it was the RIAA that certified it as such. These tasks of setting standards and monitoring sales were non-controversial and the RIAA had no enemies to speak of; the general public had probably never heard of them.

In the time since the RIAA's founding, the entire landscape of the recording industry has changed. Record labels are no longer owned or managed by musicians, producers, or other people close to the source such as the artist. The major record labels have spent the forty years since the RIAA's founding to merge, acquire, and otherwise gobble up all the independent labels that had anything in their catalog that was earning and selling. The RIAA has evolved from a group of label owners and engineers concerned with the quality of their product to a major trade association that lobbies incessantly for greater control over the public's entertainment experience. The association has gone from a quality assurance and public relations entity to the legal junk yard dog of the corporate owners.

Put bluntly, the RIAA is no longer the voice of the recording industry in terms of those who actually work in the trenches day in and day out. The RIAA is "owned" by four companies, EMI, Sony BMG Music, Universal Music Group, and the Warner Music Group. There is a long list of "members" on their Website, but many of the labels listed there are not members. The lion's share of the others are sub-labels or record companies that retained their name but are owned by corporate masters. For example, if Warner has acquired 200 record labels, they are all listed even though it is really one label we are talking about. The chairman and president are not musicians or producers; they are lawyers. The board of directors reflects only members that are executives in the afore-mentioned "Big Four." This would be like a company listing all its employees individually as the company. A member "label" owned by Warner for example would not be in an adversarial position to the parent company.

The recording industry has moved from being about the music to being about the money. Recording artists, composers, and songwriters have long been historically underrepresented at the table of fair compensation. The labels are fighting for their exclusive, world-wide, and perpetual right to screw the artist.

The major claim of the RIAA, and it is a valid one, is that the money that is due the artist is stolen from the mouth of the band by the pirating public. These hard working musicians and recording artists are denied their just compensation because of millions of Internet users stealing their intellectual property. What they don't tell you in their argument is how the present system they battle to uphold is, and I'm being kind here, less than equitable from the artist's point of view. We'll touch more on that in a minute.

The record companies are long on greed and short on vision. Had they been at the forefront of the digital revolution, leading rather than coming in late with reactionary and heavy-handed solutions that make criminals out of college dorm residents, we might be looking at DRM through lenses of a different color.

The recording industry's battle against technology is nothing new. They are always late to the game and always opposed to new technology, not because of the technology itself, but because they didn't think it out in advance and create a model that utilized the new technology to their benefit. If they embraced and even took the lead on technology (ah, the old days when they set the definition of music technology), they would have found plenty of opportunity and revenues. Instead, the RIAA took the Luddite approach and, due to their own poor planning, are now scrambling to reestablish themselves as a real player.

Much of the RIAA's problem is in perception. Everyone outside the association views them as the devil incarnate and they have earned this public image. What is their response to downloading music? Sue grandmothers and college students who are downloading and sharing files.

From the business side of the industry, one of the main reasons that the major labels are facing such financial trouble is that their model is about thirty years out of date. The following scenario is admittedly very simple and I am pulling the figures out of the sky, but the basic premise of the following is one of the prime reasons the labels have lost their right to "partner" with new artists.

BigCorp Records, after trying hard to get a 360° deal, settles for a traditional recording contract with the fabulous Today Tones. At the offset the deal looks sweet and promising to the artist.

The label promises:

▶ A recording budget of $150,000, increasing by 10 percent for two more subsequent releases should the label utilize their option for three albums over five years.

▶ A promotional budget of at least $200,000 per release.

▶ A payment of $1.00 per CD sold after they have recouped their initial investment.

▶ The moon.

The band gets:

▶ In the fine print, the label has the right to designate the producer and studio. The first thing they do is find a producer that is under their thumb in some way and book you into the most glamorous and expensive recording studio they can find—sometimes even a subsidiary business unit of the label itself.

▶ Likewise with the $200,000 promotion budget; it gets allocated to another internal division of the company or farmed out to a label buddy.

The band sees the RIAA has certified the Today Tones new release, "Bending over for Our Masters," as a platinum seller. Platinum means 1,000,000 copies sold. The band does some quick math in their heads and comes up with $1,000,000 for "each copy sold." They wait anxiously at their mailbox for the forthcoming big royalty check for their million-seller. For some reason the band never looked at the "recoup" part of the royalty schedule. Much like our jaded Nashville publisher in a previous chapter, the label pads the production, promotion, and distribution budget with payments much larger than market rate to other divisions of the company and strategic partners, so there is likely to be no "net profit" for the artist to share in. The wait at the mailbox will be a long one.

So, the music-buying public and the emerging musician rightly see the major labels not as their partner, but their adversary. A&R departments are being run by Harvard MBAs with tin ears; promotional departments are being run by people who see no difference between band branding and selling toothpaste.

These days there is only one thing that speaks to the labels: not art, not coolness or even staking out a claim on the cultural landscape, but money. The number at the bottom line of the corporate quarterly report is what will guide the company into the future. And who will be doing the guiding? More non-music professionals who know how to count beans and dream up blue sky earnings schemes that in the long term will only create more problems down the road.

The road to success has its share of challenges and pitfalls. Hopefully, you are a bit better armed at the conclusion of this book than you were at the start. Don't forget there are many more contract examples on the accompanying CD-ROM and you can drop by The Music Office Website for special extras available to those who purchase the book. I'll see you in the trenches.

APPENDIX A

Contracts, Forms, and Worksheets

Here are a few of the common forms you are likely to see on your fiscal march to fame. There are also some spreadsheet examples that will give you a better idea of how your money is being utilized at home, on the road, and in the studio.

AGREEMENT FOR SOUND CONTRACTING

Agreement made this ____ day of _____, 20___, by and between _____(Sound Company)_____ , (hereinafter referred to as the "Contractor") and _____ , (hereinafter referred to as the "Buyer") for the purpose of contracting sound reinforcement between the undersigned parties.

1.   Contractor hereby agrees to provide all the sound and lighting equipment specified in Exhibit "A", attached hereto and made a part of this Agreement. Contractor warrants that the equipment listed in Exhibit "A" is in good working order and equal to the manufacturer's operating specifications.

2.   The Contractor shall have the equipment provided for in Exhibit "A" set up and ready to operated at:

Street: _____

City: _____,State: _____, Zip: _____

Phone: _____

by _____ am/pm _____, 20___.

3.   Load-in may commence at: ____ am/pm _____, 20____.

4.   Soundcheck may commence at: __ am\pm _____, 20____

5.   Showtime is: _____ am/pm _____, 20____.

6.   The Contractor shall operate and leave the equipment set up until: _____ am/pm _____, 20____ after which the Contractor shall remove all equipment and personnel from the venue by _____ am/pm, _____, 20____.

7.   Buyer shall pay to Contractor the amount of $ _____ upon the execution of this agreement as a non-refundable deposit for Contractor's services. At the completion of soundcheck, with Contractor's equipment in place and tested, Buyer shall pay to Contractor, in U.S. currency or certified cashier's check the balance of $ _____.

8.   Contractor will provide qualified personnel to operate all equipment provided for in this Agreement. No other personnel,including Buyer and/or his employees, shall operate the Contractor's equipment without the express consent of Contractor.

9.   Buyer shall provide adequate security to protect the Contractor's equipment and personnel during the term of this Agreement. Buyer will provide the following security personnel at the following times and places:

        a)   ____ backstage security person(s) at the equipment access door during load-in

        b)   ____ security person(s) at the main mixing console fifteen (15) minutes before the public is admitted into the venue; to remain there until the public has left the venue.

        c)   ____ security person(s) at the monitor mixing console 15 minutes before the public is admitted into the venue; to remain there until the public has left the venue.

d)   ____ security person(s) in the stage area from showtime until the performance is completed, including encores.

e)   ____ security person(s) at the equipment access door during load-out.

10.   Buyer shall issue all-access permits to all designated employees of the Contractor in advance of Contractor's arrival at the venue. The personnel designated for such access are:

_____
_____
_____
_____
_____
_____

Buyer shall be notified in advance of Contractor's arrival at the venue if there are any changes in the list of Contractor's personnel required to complete the terms of this Agreement. Contractor will use only personnel directly connected to the production of the event under the terms of this Agreement.

11.   Buyer shall provide the electrical power and circuits necessary for Contractor to perform his duties hereunder. The Contractor's electrical requirements are listed in Exhibit "B"attached hereto. Buyer will use only licensed and bonded electricians in preparing the Contractor's electrical requirements. Power must be in place and of the specifications in Exhibit "B" one hour before the load-in time specified herein.

12.   Buyer will provide adequate parking immediately adjacent to the staging area for the loading and unloading of equipment and parking/vehicle access permits to Contractor and his designated vehicles. Parking shall be reserved in advance for any vehicle the Contractor may need in the performance of his duties hereunder. It is Buyer's responsibility to retain access to and from the stage area and to secure Contractor's parking during thee ntire term of this Agreement.

13.   Contractor is acting as an independent contractor in the performance of his duties herein. Buyer is not responsible for any workman compensation insurance of any kind for Contractor or Contractor's employees or personnel. All expenses pertaining to Contractor's employees and personnel, including but not limited to taxes, insurance, union or guild dues or any other expenses regarding Contractor's employees or personnel are the sole responsibility of the Contractor.

14.   This Agreement is for service rendered rain or shine. Contractor has the right to interrupt the performance of his duties hereunder in the event of inclement weather or any other conditions which Contractor or Buyer regard as hazardous to any person or persons. Any such interruption, postponement or cancellation of services shall not affect the Contractor's compensation specified herein.

15.   **ADDITIONAL TERMS AND CONDITIONS:**

See Attached Rider (if any)

16.   Should any portion of this Agreement prove to be invalid, illegal or unenforceable, it shall not affect the balance of this Agreement. This Agreement is guided by and governed by the laws of the State of _____ and _____, County shall be the place of execution and jurisdiction.

17.   Should any litigation arise between the parties hereto regarding the performance of this Agreement, the prevailing party shall be compensated for whatever damages are awarded, plus reasonable attorney's fees by the other party.

18.   This Agreement is the complete understanding between the parties and supersedes and replaces all previous agreements or representations both written and oral.

        THE UNDERSIGNED PARTIES have read and understand the terms and conditions of this Agreement and do hereby set their hands.

_____   _____
Contractor   **Buyer**
address   address
phone   phone

EXHIBIT A

INVENTORY OF EQUIPMENT AND SERVICES TO BE PROVIDED

FESTIVAL ENTERTAINMENT AGREEMENT

THIS ENTERTAINMENT AGREEMENT is made this __ day of _____, 20__ by and between _____(Buyer)_____ (hereinafter referred to as the "Buyer") and the entertainer or entertainers, if more than one, listed on Addendum A attached hereto and included herein (hereinafter referred to as the "Artist"), by and through their designated agent or representative ("Manager") identified below.

WHEREAS, Buyer conducts the annual event known as _____ (hereinafter referred to as the "Festival"); and

WHEREAS, Buyer desires to hire Artist, as independent contractor(s), to provide the entertainment generally described below (the "Performance") at the 20__ Festival; and

WHEREAS, Artist(s) desire to provide such Performance at the Festival;

NOW, THEREFORE, the parties agree as follows:

1.   **Entertainers:** The names and addresses of the Entertainers who will appear during the Performance, the amounts to be paid to each, and the Entertainer's social security numbers and union numbers, if any, are as set forth on Addendum A.

2.   **Manager:** The name and mailing address of the Manager, who is executing this Agreement on behalf of Artist(s), is:

_____
_____
_____
_____

3.   **Place of Performance:** The place of performance is at

_____

4.   **Date(s) and Time(s) of Performance:** The date(s) of the Performance shall be _____, 20__ and the time(s) of the Performance shall be _____. This Performance shall have a duration of at least _____ hours.

5.   **Performance:** The entertainment to be provided by Entertainers is generally described as:

_____

6.   **Agreement to Perform:** Artist(s) agree to provide the Performance in accordance with the terms of this Agreement and any addendums or riders hereto.

7.   **Price of Performance:** Buyer agrees to pay Artist or his agent an aggregate of _____ DOLLARS ($xxxxx.xx) for the Performance by check immediately following the Performance, which check shall be made payable to the Manager. Upon proper endorsement of such check by Manager, Buyer agrees to cash the check for the Manager. The Manager shall distribute such amount to Artist(s) as agreed upon between them.

8. **Recording, Reproduction or Transmission of Performance:** Buyer will use its best efforts to prevent the recording, reproduction or transmission of the Performance without the written permission of Artist(s) or Artist's representative.

9. **Excuse of Obligations:** Buyer and Artist shall be excused from their obligations hereunder in the event of proven sickness, accident, riot, strike, epidemic, act of God or any other legitimate condition or occurrence beyond their respective control.

10. **Taxes:** Buyer agrees to prepare and file all tax information required of a person who hires an independent contractor and Artist(s) agree that they have sole responsibility for the payment of any federal or state taxes arising from the monies paid by Buyer to Artist(s) for the Performance.

11. **Indemnify for Copyright Infringement:** Artist(s) represent and warrant that they are knowledgeable about the copyright laws of the United States as applicable to the Performance, and that Artist(s) shall not perform any copyrighted materials of others during Performance without full compliance with such applicable copyright laws. In the event that Artist(s) breach this representation, warranty and covenant, Artist(s) hereby agree to INDEMNIFY AND HOLD HARMLESS Buyer and its employees, guests and agents from and against all liability, loss, damages, claims, and expenses (including attorney's fees) arising out of such breach.

12. **Independent Contractor:** Artist(s) acknowledge that they shall perform their obligations hereunder as an independent contractor and not as an employee of Buyer. Artist(s) further acknowledge that they are not on Buyer's payroll and social security or tax withholding rolls. Artist(s) shall have sole control and direction in the conduct of the Performance.

13. **Merchandising:** Artist(s) shall not, during the 20___ Festival sell any goods, products, merchandise or services (other than the services provided herein) on the grounds of the Festival.

14. **Promotion:** Buyer shall be entitled to advertise and promote the appearance of Artist(s) at the 20___ Festival and the Performance. Artist(s) acknowledge that Buyer will rely on the terms hereof in all such promotions and advertising and in the brochures to be printed setting forth the names, dates and times of all performances to be held at the 20___ Festival. Artist(s) hereby acknowledge and agree that Buyer may use their names, photographs, likeness, facsimile signature and any other promotional materials in all of such promotions, advertising or other activities used to increase attendance at the 20___ Festival.

15. **Parking:** Buyer shall provide parking space for vehicles in a location of close proximity to and with direct access to the backstage area where Performance will take place on the date(s) of Performance. This parking space will be reserved for Artist(s) for a period of four (4) hours prior to the Performance and ending three (3) hours following the Performance.

16. **Security:** Buyer shall provide security for the backstage and stage areas before, during and after the Performance. Buyer shall provide security personnel to protect Artist(s) and their property as deemed appropriate by Buyer in its discretion.

17. **Passes:** Buyer shall provide identification passes to Artist(s) for the backstage and stage where Performance is to be held.

18. **Stage:** At its sole expense, Buyer shall furnish the stage, and stage lighting, sound and power for the Performance, and Buyer shall provide all stagehands required to assist the setup for and conduct of the Performance and takedown after the Performance.

19.　　**Dressing Rooms:** Buyer shall provide Artist(s) with one private dressing room, which will be clean, dry, well lit and air conditioned.

20.　　**Authority to Execute:** The Manager who is executing this Agreement on behalf of Artist(s) hereby warrants and represents that he has the full power and authority to bind Artist(s) on whose behalf he is executing this Agreement and acknowledges that he is making this representation and warranty with the understanding that Buyer is relying thereon.

　　IN WITNESS WHEREOF, this Agreement is executed on the date first above written.

BUYER

By:

MANAGER

By:

Title:

ADDENDUM A
List of Artist(s)

NAMES & ADDRESSES OF ENTERTAINERS　　　　　SOCIAL SECURITY/UNION NO.

_____　　　　_____
_____

_____　　　　_____
_____

_____　　　　_____
_____

_____　　　　_____
_____

_____　　　　_____
_____

Commercial Music Contract

THIS AGREEMENT is for the services described below between the undersigned purchaser (hereinafter referred to as "PURCHASER") and the undersigned licensor (hereinafter referred to as "LICENSOR").

1. The LICENSOR hereby agrees to produce and deliver to the PURCHASER the following radio/television commercial package under the following terms and conditions:

    (a) The musical style of the commercial package desired by the PURCHASER is described as:

_____

_____

_____

    (b) The vocal style most desired by the PURCHASER can be generally described as:

_____

_____

_____

    (c) The length(s) of the Commercial(s) most desired by the PURCHASER is _____ seconds long.

    (d) The recommended lyrics or voice-over for the Commercial Package are as follows:
        Introduction:

_____

_____

_____

_____

Bed:

_____

_____

_____

_____

Exit:

_____

_____

_____

_____

Additional Notes:

_____

_____

_____

_____

2. LICENSOR agrees to produce and deliver to the PURCHASER the commercial(s) stated above within thirty (30) days.

3. LICENSOR agrees to follow as closely as possible the outlines stated above for production style and copy.

4. LICENSOR shall retain all rights and copyrights to the music, melody and lyrics to the commercial. The use of the music, melody and lyrics is only to be leased to the PURCHASER for the territory specified for the term of this agreement.

5. LICENSOR hereby warrants and represents that the music, melody, and lyrics of the commercial is new and original and does not infringe on the rights or copyrights of others. LICENSOR further agrees to defend PURCHASER against any proceedings against him for copyright infringement. All costs of any such legal proceedings will be the LICENSOR'S responsibility.

6. LICENSOR agrees not to license the music, melody or lyrics for this particular commercial to any other person, firm or corporation within a radius of One Hundred (100) Miles of the PURCHASER'S broadcast center. This broadcast center is defined as

_____.

7. PURCHASER agrees not to broadcast or otherwise use the performance embodied in the commercial for any other market or region outside the aforementioned broadcast center without the express written approval of LICENSOR.

8. LICENSOR agrees to provide PURCHASER, at no additional cost, one reel-to-reel (7½ ips) version and one compact disc version of the commercial package. Additional copies may be purchased at the following rate:

        (a) Reel-to-real copies: $ _____ each
        (b) Cassette copies: $ _____ each
        (c) CD copies: $ _____ each

9. The term "commercial package" as used herein is defined as the following:
        (a) One thirty second version with no vocals
        (b) One thirty second version with intro vocals
        (c) One thirty second version with outro vocals
        (d) One thirty second version with intro and outro vocals
        (e) One thirty second version with full vocals
        (f) One sixty second version with no vocals
        (g) One sixty second version with intro vocals
        (h) One sixty second version with outro vocals
        (i) One sixty second version with intro and outro vocals
        (j) One sixty second version with full vocals

10. Transfer, sale or reassignment of this lease by PURCHASER is strictly forbidden without the written express consent of LICENSOR.

11. LICENSOR has the option at any time during the initial term of this Agreement to purchase from the LICENSOR all rights and copyrights to the music, melody and lyrics of this particular musical commercial. The purchase price of said rights shall be $_____. Upon payment of this amount, LICENSOR will relinquish and release to PURCHASER all rights and copyrights worldwide to the performance and ownership.

12. Payment of LICENSOR by PURCHASER for the commercial package herein shall be as follows:

      (a) A deposit of $ _____ shall be paid to LICENSOR at the time of execution of this Agreement.

      (b)The balance due LICENSOR shall be paid within Ten (10) days of the delivery and receipt by PURCHASER of the completed commercial package.

13. The agreed upon price of the commercial package is $_____ per year. This fee is for the exclusive right to use and re-use the commercial package for the specific area mentioned in Section 4 of this Agreement. This price is exclusive of sales tax or any other taxes due and payable from the sale of this license.

14. Governing Law: This Agreement shall be governed by the laws and in the courts of the State of _____ and by the laws of the United States, excluding their conflicts of law principles. Any dispute or legal proceeding regarding the Agreement shall take place in the county of _____, in the State of _____.

Dated: _____

For PURCHASER: _____

For LICENSOR : _____

MUSIC BUSINESS CONTRACTS
Musician Personal Inventory

Please list your equipment and value below:

If you need more space under a given category, paste in a new row under that category but above the Total formula for the category.

SUMMARY	Fair Value
Sound Equipment	
Musical Instruments	
Vehicles	
Computer Equipment	
Office Equipment	
Recording/Other Equipment	
Misc.	
Total Inventory Value	

ITEMIZATION			
SOUND EQUIPMENT			
Microphones	*Brand/Model*	*Serial #*	**Fair Value**
Total Microphones			
Amplifier(s)	*Brand/Model*	*Serial #*	**Fair Value**
Total Amplifiers			
Mixer(s)	*Brand/Model*	*Serial #*	**Fair Value**
Total Mixers			
Cable (mike, line and speaker)	*Brand/Model*	*Serial #*	**Fair Value**
Total Cable			
Microphone stands	*Brand/Model*	*Serial #*	**Fair Value**
Total Mic Stands			
Cases	*Brand/Model*	*Serial #*	**Fair Value**
Total Cases			

Outboard Gear/Misc.	Brand/Model	Serial #	Fair Value
Total Outboard Gear Misc.			
TOTAL SOUND EQUIPMENT			

MUSICAL INSTRUMENTS			
Stringed Instruments	Brand/Model	Serial #	Fair Value
Total Stringed Instruments			
Keyboards/Electronics	Brand/Model	Serial #	Fair Value
Total Keyboards/Electronics			
Drums/Percussion	Brand/Model	Serial #	Fair Value
Total Drums/Percussion			
Brass Instruments	Brand/Model	Serial #	Fair Value
Total Brass Instruments			
Instruments/Misc.	Brand/Model	Serial #	Fair Value
Total Instruments/Misc.			
TOTAL MUSICAL INSTRUMENTS			

VEHICLES/TRAILERS	Brand/Model	Serial #	Fair Value
TOTAL VEHICLES			

COMPUTER EQUIPMENT			
Hardware	Brand/Model	Serial #	Fair Value

Software	Brand/Model	Serial #	Fair Value
TOTAL COMPUTER EQUIPMENT			

OFFICE EQUIPMENT	Brand/Model	Serial #	Fair Value
TOTAL OFFICE EQUIPMENT			

RECORDING/OTHER EQUIPMENT	Brand/Model	Serial #	Fair Value
TOTAL OTHER EQUIPMENT			

MISC.	Brand/Model	Serial #	Fair Value
TOTAL MISC.			

MUSIC BUSINESS CONTRACTS		
DAILY INCOME AND EXPENSE REPORT		
Artist Name:		
Date:		
Location:		
* note all reimbursements are for RECEIPTED expenses only!		

SUMMARY		AMOUNT
Income		
Expense		
DAILY NET		

INCOME	SOURCE	AMOUNT
Performance Fees		
Merchandising		
Other		
TOTAL INCOME		

EXPENSES	LOCATION	AMOUNT
Hotel		
Vehicle		
Travel		
Fuel		
Equipment		
Per Diem		
Tolls/Permits/Taxes		
Other Expenses		
TOTAL EXPENSES		

REPORT DETAIL		
INCOME	NOTES	AMOUNT
PERFORMANCE		
Performance Fees		
Misc.		
TOTAL PERFORMANCE		
MERCHANDISING	NOTES	AMOUNT
CDs		
Cassettes		
T-shirts		
Caps		
Other		
TOTAL MERCHANDISE		
OTHER INCOME	SOURCE	AMOUNT
TOTAL OTHER INCOME		
EXPENSES		
HOTEL/LODGING	LOCATION	AMOUNT
Hotel		
Parking		

Meals		
Cleaning		
Phone		
Tips/Misc.		
TOTAL HOTEL		
VEHICLE	**ITEM**	**AMOUNT**
Parts/Tires		
Repairs		
Rental		
Insurance		
Tax/Misc.		
TOTAL VEHICLE		
TRAVEL	**ITEM**	**AMOUNT**
Tickets		
Taxi/Transport		
Baggage Fees		
Tips/Misc.		
TOTAL TRAVEL		
FUEL	**ITEM**	**AMOUNT**
Gas/Diesel		
Oil		
Other		
TOTAL FUEL		
EQUIPMENT	**ITEM**	**AMOUNT**
Repairs		
Strings/Sticks		
Lights		
Tape		
Misc.		
TOTAL EQUIPMENT		
PER DIEM		
Road Manager		
Sound Man		
Band Member 1		
Band Member 2		
Band Member 3		
Band Member 4		
Band Member 5		
TOTAL PER DIEM		
TOLLS/TAXES	**ITEM**	**AMOUNT**
Road Tolls		
Permits		
Other		
TOTAL TOLLS/TAXES		
OTHER EXPENSES	**ITEMIZE**	**AMOUNT**
Misc.		
TOTAL MISC. EXPENSES		

APPENDIX B

Professional Associations, Unions, and Guilds

Your career will have you bumping into many of these pro organizations. From the AFM to SESAC, your participation with one of these associations is almost assured at some point during your career. Here is a list of the major players.

American Society of Composers, Authors & Publishers (ASCAP)
ASCAP Building
One Lincoln Plaza
New York, NY 10023
Telephone: (800) 99-ASCAP, Fax: (800) FX-ASCAP
Website: www.ascap.com

Broadcast Music Incorporated (BMI)
10 Music Square East
Nashville, TN 37203
Telephone: (615) 401-2473, Fax: (212) 489-2368
Website: www.bmi.com

SESAC, Inc.
421 West 54th Street
New York, NY 10019-4405
Telephone: (212) 586-3450, Fax: (212) 489-5699
Website: www.sesac.com

The Harry Fox Agency, Inc.
711 Third Ave.
New York, NY 10017
Telephone: (212) 370-5330, Fax: (212) 953-2384
Website: www.nmpa.org

American Federation of Musicians, (AFM)
1501 Broadway
Suite 600
New York, NY 10036
Telephone: (212) 869-1330, Fax: (212) 764-6134
Website: www.afm.org

International Alliance of Theatrical Stage Employees, Moving Picture Technicians, Artists and Allied Crafts of the United States, (IATSE)
1430 Broadway
20th Floor
New York, NY 10018
Telephone: 212-730-1770
Website: www.iatse-intl.org

Association of Talent Agents (ATA)
9255 Sunset Blvd.
Suite 930
Los Angeles, CA 90069
(310) 274-0628, Fax (310) 274-5063
Website: www.agentassociation.com

National Association of Recording Industry Professionals (NARIP)
Post Office Box 2446
Toluca Lake, CA 91610-2446
Phone: (818) 769-7007
Email: info@narip.com

National Academy of Recording Arts and Sciences (NARAS)
The Recording Academy
3402 Pico Blvd.
Santa Monica, CA 90405
Phone: (310) 392-3777, Fax: (310) 399-3090

The GRAMMY Foundation
3402 Pico Blvd.
Santa Monica, CA 90405
Telephone: (310) 392-3777
Fax: (310) 392-2188
Website: www.grammy.com

The Essential Forms

Y ou can find more Library of Congress forms on the CD-ROM or you can always surf to http://www.copyright. gov for the latest versions. The two most commonly used forms: FORM PA and FORM SR are on the following pages.

FORM PA is the form you will use to copyright a single song or compilation of songs.

FORM SR is for copyrighting a sound recording. Use this for all your audio recordings that may see the public light of day.

Instructions for Short Form PA

For works in the performing arts (except audiovisual works)

USE THIS FORM IF—

1. You are the *only* author and copyright owner of this work, *and*
2. The work was *not* made for hire, *and*
3. The work is completely new (does not contain a substantial amount of material that has been previously published or registered or is in the public domain) and is not an audiovisual work.

If any of the above does not apply, you must use standard Form PA.

NOTE: *Short Form PA is not appropriate for an anonymous author who does not wish to reveal his or her identity and may not be used for audiovisual works, including motion pictures.*

HOW TO COMPLETE SHORT FORM PA

- Type or print in black ink.
- Be clear and legible. (Your certificate of registration will be copied from your form.)
- Give only the information requested.

NOTE: You may use a continuation sheet (Form CON) to list individual titles in a collection. Complete Space A and list the individual titles under Space C on the back page. Space B is not applicable to short forms.

1 Title of This Work

You must give a title. If there is no title, state "UNTITLED." Alternative title: If the work is known by two titles, you also may give the second title. Or if the work has been published as part of a larger work, give the title of that larger work, in addition to the title of the contribution.

If you are registering an unpublished collection, give the collection title you want to appear in our records (for example: "Songs by Alice, Volume 1"). Be sure to keep a personal record of the songs you have included in the collection. If you want the certificate of registration to list the individual titles as well as the collection title, use a continuation sheet (Form___/CON).

2 Name and Address of Author and Owner of the Copyright

Give your name and mailing address. You may include your pseudonym followed by "pseud." Also, give the nation of which you are a citizen or where you have your domicile (i.e., permanent residence). Give daytime phone and fax numbers and email address, if available.

3 Year of Creation

Give the latest year in which you completed the work you are registering at this time. A work is "created" when it is written down, recorded, or otherwise "fixed" in a tangible form.

4 Publication

If the work has been published (i.e., if copies have been distributed to the public), give the complete date of publication (month, day, and year) and the nation where the publication first took place.

5 Type of Authorship in This Work

Check the box or boxes that describe the kind of material you are registering. Check *only* the authorship included in the copy, tape, or CD you are sending with the application. For example, if you are registering lyrics and plan to add music later, check only the box for "lyrics."

6 Signature of Author

Sign the application in black ink and check the appropriate box. The person signing the application should be the author or his/her authorized agent.

7 Person to Contact for Rights and Permissions

This space is optional. You may give the name and address of the person or organization to contact for permission to use the work. You may also provide phone, fax, or email information.

8 Certificate Will Be Mailed

This space must be completed. Your certificate of registration will be mailed in a window envelope to this address. Also, if the Copyright Office needs to contact you, we will write to this address.

9 Deposit Account

Complete this space only if you currently maintain a deposit account in the Copyright Office.

MAIL WITH THE FORM—

- The filing fee, in the form of a check or money order (*no cash*) payable to *Register of Copyrights*, and
- One or two copies of the work. If the work is unpublished, send one copy, tape, or CD. If published, send two copies of the best published edition if the work is in printed form, such as sheet music, or one copy of the best published edition if the work is recorded on a tape or disk.

Note: Inquire about special requirements for works first published outside the United States or before 1978. Copies submitted become the property of the U.S. Government.

Mail everything (application form, copy or copies, and fee) *in one package* to: *Library of Congress, Copyright Office, 101 Independence Avenue SE, Washington, DC 20559-6000*

Questions? Call (202) 707-3000 between 8:30 a.m. and 5:00 p.m. eastern time, Monday through Friday, except federal holidays. For forms and informational circulars, call (202) 707-9100 24 hours a day, 7 days a week, or download them at *www.copyright.gov.*

Copyright Office fees are subject to change. For current fees, check the Copyright Office website at *www.copyright.gov*, write the Copyright Office, or call (202) 707-3000.

For best results, fill in the form on-screen and then print it.

Short Form PA
For a Work of Performing Arts
UNITED STATES COPYRIGHT OFFICE

REGISTRATION NUMBER

_____

PA _____ PAU _____

Effective Date of Registration

_____

Application Received

_____

Deposit Received
One | Two

Examined By

Correspondence ❑

Fee Received

TYPE OR PRINT IN BLACK INK. DO NOT WRITE ABOVE THIS LINE.

1 **Title of This Work:**

Alternative title or title of larger work in which this work was published:

2 **Name and Address of Author and Owner of the Copyright:**

Nationality or domicile:
Phone, fax, and email:

Phone ( ) Fax ( )
Email:

3 **Year of Creation:**

4 **If work has been published, Date and Nation of Publication:**

a. Date _____ _____ _____ *(Month, day, and*
Month Day Year *year all required)*

b. Nation

5 **Type of Authorship in This Work:**

Check all that this author created.

❑ Music ❑ Other text (includes dramas, screenplays, etc.)
❑ Lyrics *(If your work is a motion picture or other audiovisual work, use the standard Form PA.)*

6 **Signature:**
(Registration cannot be completed without a signature.)

I certify that the statements made by me in this application are correct to the best of my knowledge. Check one:

❑ Author
❑ Authorized agent **X**_____

OPTIONAL

7 **Name and Address of Person to Contact for Rights and Permissions:**

Phone, fax, and email:

❑ Check here if same as #2 above.

Phone ( ) Fax ( )
Email:

8
Certificate will be mailed in window envelope to this address:

Name ▼

Number/Street/Apt ▼

City/State/Zip ▼

Complete this space only if you currently hold a deposit account in the Copyright Office.

9 Deposit account #_____

Name _____

_____

_____

DO NOT WRITE HERE Page 1 of _____ pages

*17 USC §506(e): Any person who knowingly makes a false representation of a material fact in the application for copyright registration provided for by section 409, or in any written statement filed in connection with the application, shall be fined not more than $2,500.

Form PA-Short Rev: 04/2007 Print: 04/2007—xx,000 Printed on recycled paper

U.S. Government Printing Office: 2007-xxx-xxx/60,xxx

Page 2 of 2

Form SR

Detach and read these instructions before completing this form.
Make sure all applicable spaces have been filled in before you return this form.

When to Use This Form: Use Form SR for registration of published or unpublished sound recordings. It should be used when the copyright claim is limited to the sound recording itself, and it may also be used where the same copyright claimant is seeking simultaneous registration of the underlying musical, dramatic, or literary work embodied in the phonorecord.

With one exception, "sound recordings" are works that result from the fixation of a series of musical, spoken, or other sounds. The exception is for the audio portions of audiovisual works, such as a motion picture soundtrack or an audio cassette accompanying a filmstrip. These are considered a part of the audiovisual work as a whole.

Deposit to Accompany Application: An application for copyright registration must be accompanied by a deposit consisting of phonorecords representing the entire work for which registration is to be made.

Unpublished Work: Deposit one complete phonorecord.

Published Work: Deposit two complete phonorecords of the best edition, together with "any printed or other visually perceptible material" published with the phonorecords.

Work First Published Outside the United States: Deposit one complete phonorecord of the first foreign edition.

Contribution to a Collective Work: Deposit one complete phonorecord of the best edition of the collective work.

The Copyright Notice: Before March 1, 1989, the use of copyright notice was mandatory on all published works, and any work first published before that date should have carried a notice. For works first published on and after March 1, 1989, use of the copyright notice is optional. For more information about copyright notice, see Circular 3, *Copyright Notices*.

For Further Information: To speak to a Copyright Office staff member, call (202) 707-3000 (TTY: (202) 707-6737). Recorded information is available 24 hours a day. Order forms and other publications from Library of Congress, Copyright Office, 101 Independence Avenue SE, Washington, DC 20559-6000 or call the Forms and Publications Hotline at (202) 707-9100. Access and download circulars, forms, and other information from the Copyright Office website at *www.copyright.gov*.

Please type or print neatly using black ink. The form is used to produce the certificate.

SPACE 1: Title

Title of This Work: Every work submitted for copyright registration must be given a title to identify that particular work. If the phonorecords or any accompanying printed material bears a title (or an identifying phrase that could serve as a title), transcribe that wording completely and exactly on the application. Indexing of the registration and future identification of the work may depend on the information you give here.

Previous, Alternative, or Contents Titles: Complete this space if there are any previous or alternative titles for the work under which someone searching for the registration might be likely to look, or under which a document pertaining to the work might be recorded. You may also give the individual contents titles, if any, in this space or you may use a Continuation Sheet. Circle the term that describes the titles given.

SPACE 2: Author(s)

General Instructions: After reading these instructions, decide who are the "authors" of this work for copyright purposes. Then, unless the work is a "collective work," give the requested information about every "author" who contributed any appreciable amount of copyrightable matter to this version of the work. If you need further space, request additional Continuation Sheets. In the case of a collective work such as a collection of previously published or registered sound recordings, give information about the author of the collective work as a whole. If you are submitting this Form SR to cover the recorded musical, dramatic, or literary work as well as the sound recording itself, it is important for space 2 to include full information about the various authors of all of the material covered by the copyright claim, making clear the nature of each author's contribution.

Name of Author: The fullest form of the author's name should be given. Unless the work was "made for hire," the individual who actually created the work is its "author." In the case of a work made for hire, the statute provides that "the employer or other person for whom the work was prepared is considered the author."

What Is a "Work Made for Hire"? A "work made for hire" is defined as: (1) "a work prepared by an employee within the scope of his or her employment"; or (2) "a work specially ordered or commissioned for use as a contribution to a collective work, as a part of a motion picture or other audiovisual work, as a translation, as a supplementary work, as a compilation, as an instructional text, as a test, as answer material for a test, or as an atlas, if the parties expressly agree in a written instrument signed by them that the work shall be considered a work made for hire." If you have checked "Yes" to indicate that the work was "made for hire," you must give the full legal name of the employer (or other person for whom the work was prepared). You may also include the name of the employee along with the name of the employer (for example: "Elster Record Co., employer for hire of John Ferguson").

"Anonymous" or "Pseudonymous" Work: An author's contribution to a work is "anonymous" if that author is not identified on the copies or phonorecords of the work. An author's contribution to a work is "pseudonymous" if that author is identified on the copies or phonorecords under a fictitious name. If the work is "anonymous" you may: (1) leave the line blank; or (2) state "anonymous" on the line; or (3) reveal the author's identity. If the work is "pseudonymous" you may: (1) leave the line blank; or (2) give the pseudonym and identify it as such (for example: "Huntley Haverstock, pseudonym"); or (3) reveal the author's name, making clear which is the real name and which is the pseudonym (for example: "Judith Barton, whose pseudonym is Madeline Elster"). However, the citizenship or domicile of the author *must* be given in all cases.

Dates of Birth and Death: If the author is dead, the statute requires that the year of death be included in the application unless the work is anonymous or pseudonymous. The author's birth date is optional, but is useful as a form of identification. Leave this space blank if the author's contribution was a "work made for hire."

Author's Nationality or Domicile: Give the country in which the author is a citizen, or the country in which the author is domiciled. Nationality or domicile *must* be given in all cases.

Nature of Authorship: Sound recording authorship is the performance, sound production, or both, that is fixed in the recording deposited for registration. Describe this authorship in space 2 as "sound recording." If the claim also covers the underlying work(s), include the appropriate authorship terms for each author, for example, "words," "music," "arrangement of music," or "text."

Generally, for the claim to cover both the sound recording and the underlying work(s), every author should have contributed to both the sound recording *and* the underlying work(s). If the claim includes artwork or photographs, include the appropriate term in the statement of authorship.

Page 1 of 4

3 SPACE 3: Creation and Publication

General Instructions: Do not confuse "creation" with "publication." Every application for copyright registration must state "the year in which creation of the work was completed." Give the date and nation of first publication only if the work has been published.

Creation: Under the statute, a work is "created" when it is fixed in a copy or phonorecord for the first time. Where a work has been prepared over a period of time, the part of the work existing in fixed form on a particular date constitutes the created work on that date. The date you give here should be the year in which the author completed the particular version for which registration is now being sought, even if other versions exist or if further changes or additions are planned.

Publication: The statute defines "publication" as "the distribution of copies or phonorecords of a work to the public by sale or other transfer of ownership, or by rental, lease, or lending"; a work is also "published" if there has been an "offering to distribute copies or phonorecords to a group of persons for purposes of further distribution, public performance, or public display." Give the full date (month, date, year) when, and the country where, publication first occurred. If first publication took place simultaneously in the United States and other countries, it is sufficient to state "U.S.A."

4 SPACE 4: Claimant(s)

Name(s) and Address(es) of Copyright Claimant(s): Give the name(s) and address(es) of the copyright claimant(s) in the work even if the claimant is the same as the author. Copyright in a work belongs initially to the author of the work (including, in the case of a work made for hire, the employer or other person for whom the work was prepared). The copyright claimant is either the author of the work or a person or organization to whom the copyright initially belonging to the author has been transferred.

Transfer: The statute provides that, if the copyright claimant is not the author, the application for registration must contain "a brief statement of how the claimant obtained ownership of the copyright." If any copyright claimant named in space 4a is not an author named in space 2, give a brief statement explaining how the claimant(s) obtained ownership of the copyright. Examples: "By written contract"; "Transfer of all rights by author"; "Assignment"; "By will." Do not attach transfer documents or other attachments or riders.

5 SPACE 5: Previous Registration

General Instructions: The questions in space 5 are intended to show whether an earlier registration has been made for this work and, if so, whether there is any basis for a new registration. As a rule, only one basic copyright registration can be made for the same version of a particular work.

Same Version: If this version is substantially the same as the work covered by a previous registration, a second registration is not generally possible unless: (1) the work has been registered in unpublished form and a second registration is now being sought to cover this first published edition; or (2) someone other than the author is identified as copyright claimant in the earlier registration and the author is now seeking registration in his or her own name. If either of these two exceptions applies, check the appropriate box and give the earlier registration number and date. Otherwise, do not submit Form SR. Instead, write the Copyright Office for information about supplementary registration or recordation of transfers of copyright ownership.

Changed Version: If the work has been changed and you are now seeking reg-

istration to cover the additions or revisions, check the last box in space 5, give the earlier registration number and date, and complete both parts of space 6 in accordance with the instructions below.

Previous Registration Number and Date: If more than one previous registration has been made for the work, give the number and date of the latest registration.

6 SPACE 6: Derivative Work or Compilation

General Instructions: Complete space 6 if this work is a "changed version," "compilation," or "derivative work," and if it incorporates one or more earlier works that have already been published or registered for copyright, or that have fallen into the public domain, or sound recordings that were fixed before February 15, 1972. A "compilation" is defined as "a work formed by the collection and assembling of preexisting materials or of data that are selected, coordinated, or arranged in such a way that the resulting work as a whole constitutes an original work of authorship." A "derivative work" is "a work based on one or more preexisting works." Examples of derivative works include recordings reissued with substantial editorial revisions or abridgments of the recorded sounds, and recordings republished with new recorded material, or "any other form in which a work may be recast, transformed, or adapted." Derivative works also include works "consisting of editorial revisions, annotations, or other modifications" if these changes, as a whole, represent an original work of authorship.

Preexisting Material (space 6a): Complete this space *and* space 6b for derivative works. In this space identify the preexisting work that has been recast, transformed, or adapted. The preexisting work may be material that has been previously published, previously registered, or that is in the public domain. For example, the preexisting material might be: "1970 recording by Sperryville Symphony of Bach Double Concerto."

Material Added to This Work (space 6b): Give a brief, general statement of the **additional** new material covered by the copyright claim for which registration is sought. In the case of a derivative work, identify this new material. Examples: "Recorded performances on bands 1 and 3"; "Remixed sounds from original multitrack sound sources"; "New words, arrangement, and additional sounds." If the work is a compilation, give a brief, general statement describing both the material that has been compiled *and* the compilation itself. Example: "Compilation of 1938 Recordings by various swing bands."

7, 8, 9 SPACE 7, 8, 9: Fee, Correspondence, Certification, Return Address

Deposit Account: If you maintain a Deposit Account in the Copyright Office, identify it in space 7a. Otherwise, leave the space blank and send the filing fee with your application and deposit. (See space 8 on form.) **(Note:** Copyright Office fees are subject to change. For current fees, check the Copyright Office website at *www.copyright.gov*, write the Copyright Office, or call (202) 707-3000.)

Correspondence (space 7b): Give the name, address, area code, telephone number, fax number, and email address (if available) of the person to be consulted if correspondence about this application becomes necessary.

Certification (space 8): This application cannot be accepted unless it bears the date and the *handwritten signature* of the author or other copyright claimant, or of the owner of exclusive right(s), or of the duly authorized agent of the author, claimant, or owner of exclusive right(s).

Address for Return of Certificate (space 9): The address box must be completed legibly since the certificate will be returned in a window envelope.

▓▓▓ MORE INFORMATION ▓▓▓

"Works": "Works" are the basic subject matter of copyright; they are what authors create and copyright protects. The statute draws a sharp distinction between the "work" and "any material object in which the work is embodied."

"Copies" and "Phonorecords": These are the two types of material objects in which "works" are embodied. In general, "copies" are objects from which a work can be read or visually perceived, directly or with the aid of a machine or device, such as manuscripts, books, sheet music, film, and videotape. "Phonorecords" are objects embodying fixations of sounds, such as audio tapes and phonograph disks. For example, a song (the "work") can be reproduced in sheet music ("copies") or phonograph disks ("phonorecords"), or both.

"Sound Recordings": These are "works," not "copies" or "phonorecords." "Sound recordings" are "works that result from the fixation of a series of musical, spoken, or other sounds, but not including the sounds accompanying a motion picture or other audiovisual work." Example: When a record company issues a new release, the release will typically involve two distinct "works": the "musical work" that has been recorded, and the "sound recording" as a separate work in itself. The material objects that the record company sends out are "phonorecords": physical reproductions of both the "musical work" and the "sound recording."

Should You File More Than One Application? If your work consists of a recorded musical, dramatic, or literary work and if both that "work" and the sound recording as a separate "work" are eligible for registration, the application form you should file depends on the following:

File Only Form SR if: The copyright claimant is the same for both the musical, dramatic, or literary work and for the sound recording, and you are seeking a single registration to cover both of these "works."

File Only Form PA (or Form TX) if: You are seeking to register only the musical, dramatic, or literary work, not the sound recording. Form PA is appropriate for works of the performing arts; Form TX is for nondramatic literary works.

Separate Applications Should Be Filed on Form PA (or Form TX) and on Form SR if: (1) The copyright claimant for the musical, dramatic, or literary work is different from the copyright claimant for the sound recording; or (2) You prefer to have separate registrations for the musical, dramatic, or literary work and for the sound recording.

Form SR

For best results, fill in the form on-screen and then print it.

◉ Form SR
For a Sound Recording
UNITED STATES COPYRIGHT OFFICE

REGISTRATION NUMBER

_____

SR   SRU

EFFECTIVE DATE OF REGISTRATION

_____

Month   Day   Year

DO NOT WRITE ABOVE THIS LINE. IF YOU NEED MORE SPACE, USE A SEPARATE CONTINUATION SHEET.

1

TITLE OF THIS WORK ▼

_____

PREVIOUS, ALTERNATIVE, OR CONTENTS TITLES (CIRCLE ONE) ▼

_____

2

a

NAME OF AUTHOR ▼

DATES OF BIRTH AND DEATH
Year Born ▼   Year Died ▼

Was this contribution to the work a "work made for hire"?
☐ Yes
☐ No

AUTHOR'S NATIONALITY OR DOMICILE
Name of Country
OR { Citizen of ▶_____
     Domiciled in ▶_____

WAS THIS AUTHOR'S CONTRIBUTION TO THE WORK
Anonymous?   ☐ Yes ☐ No
Pseudonymous?   ☐ Yes ☐ No

If the answer to either of these questions is "Yes," see detailed instructions.

NATURE OF AUTHORSHIP Briefly describe nature of material created by this author in which copyright is claimed. ▼

NOTE

Under the law, the "author" of a "work made for hire" is generally the employer, not the employee (see instructions). For any part of this work that was "made for hire," check "Yes" in the space provided, give the employer (or other person for whom the work was prepared) as "Author" of that part, and leave the space for dates of birth and death blank.

b

NAME OF AUTHOR ▼

DATES OF BIRTH AND DEATH
Year Born ▼   Year Died ▼

Was this contribution to the work a "work made for hire"?
☐ Yes
☐ No

AUTHOR'S NATIONALITY OR DOMICILE
Name of Country
OR { Citizen of ▶_____
     Domiciled in ▶_____

WAS THIS AUTHOR'S CONTRIBUTION TO THE WORK
Anonymous?   ☐ Yes ☐ No
Pseudonymous?   ☐ Yes ☐ No

If the answer to either of these questions is "Yes," see detailed instructions.

NATURE OF AUTHORSHIP Briefly describe nature of material created by this author in which copyright is claimed. ▼

c

NAME OF AUTHOR ▼

DATES OF BIRTH AND DEATH
Year Born ▼   Year Died ▼

Was this contribution to the work a "work made for hire"?
☐ Yes
☐ No

AUTHOR'S NATIONALITY OR DOMICILE
Name of Country
OR { Citizen of ▶_____
     Domiciled in ▶_____

WAS THIS AUTHOR'S CONTRIBUTION TO THE WORK
Anonymous?   ☐ Yes ☐ No
Pseudonymous?   ☐ Yes ☐ No

If the answer to either of these questions is "Yes," see detailed instructions.

NATURE OF AUTHORSHIP Briefly describe nature of material created by this author in which copyright is claimed. ▼

3

a

YEAR IN WHICH CREATION OF THIS WORK WAS COMPLETED

_____ ◀ Year

This information must be given in all cases.

b

DATE AND NATION OF FIRST PUBLICATION OF THIS PARTICULAR WORK

Complete this information ONLY if this work has been published.

Month ▶ _____ Day ▶ _____ Year ▶ _____

_____ ◀ Nation

4

a

COPYRIGHT CLAIMANT(S) Name and address must be given even if the claimant is the same as the author given in space 2. ▼

_____

b

TRANSFER If the claimant(s) named here in space 4 is (are) different from the author(s) named in space 2, give a brief statement of how the claimant(s) obtained ownership of the copyright. ▼

See instructions before completing this space.

DO NOT WRITE HERE OFFICE USE ONLY

APPLICATION RECEIVED

ONE DEPOSIT RECEIVED

TWO DEPOSITS RECEIVED

FUNDS RECEIVED

MORE ON BACK ▶
· Complete all applicable spaces (numbers 5-9) on the reverse side of this page.
· See detailed instructions.   · Sign the form at line 8.

DO NOT WRITE HERE
Page 1 of _____ pages

EXAMINED BY	FORM SR
CHECKED BY	
CORRESPONDENCE	FOR COPYRIGHT OFFICE USE ONLY
❏ Yes	

DO NOT WRITE ABOVE THIS LINE. IF YOU NEED MORE SPACE, USE A SEPARATE CONTINUATION SHEET.

PREVIOUS REGISTRATION Has registration for this work, or for an earlier version of this work, already been made in the Copyright Office?

❏ Yes ❏ No If your answer is "Yes," why is another registration being sought? (Check appropriate box) ▼

a. ❏ This work was previously registered in unpublished form and now has been published for the first time.

b. ❏ This is the first application submitted by this author as copyright claimant.

c. ❏ This is a changed version of the work, as shown by space 6 on this application.

If your answer is "Yes," give: **Previous Registration Number** ▼   **Year of Registration** ▼

5

DERIVATIVE WORK OR COMPILATION

Preexisting Material Identify any preexisting work or works that this work is based on or incorporates. ▼

a

Material Added to This Work Give a brief, general statement of the material that has been added to this work and in which copyright is claimed. ▼

b

6

See instructions before completing this space.

DEPOSIT ACCOUNT If the registration fee is to be charged to a deposit account established in the Copyright Office, give name and number of Account.

Name ▼   **Account Number** ▼

a

CORRESPONDENCE Give name and address to which correspondence about this application should be sent. Name/Address/Apt/City/State/Zip ▼

b

Area code and daytime telephone number   Fax number

Email

7

CERTIFICATION* I, the undersigned, hereby certify that I am the

Check only one ▼

❏ author   ❏ owner of exclusive right(s)

❏ other copyright claimant   ❏ authorized agent of _____

Name of author or other copyright claimant, or owner of exclusive right(s) ▲

of the work identified in this application and that the statements made by me in this application are correct to the best of my knowledge.

Typed or printed name and date ▼ If this application gives a date of publication in space 3, do not sign and submit it before that date.

_____   Date _____

Handwritten signature ▼

_____

8

Certificate will be mailed in window envelope to this address	Name ▼	YOU MUST: • Complete all necessary spaces • Sign your application in space 8
	Number/Street/Apt ▼	SEND ALL 3 ELEMENTS IN THE SAME PACKAGE: 1. Application form 2. Nonrefundable filing fee in check or money order payable to *Register of Copyrights* 3. Deposit material
	City/State/Zip ▼	MAIL TO: Library of Congress Copyright Office 101 Independence Avenue SE Washington, DC 20559-6000

9

*17 *USC* §506(e): Any person who knowingly makes a false representation of a material fact in the application for copyright registration provided for by section 409, or in any written statement filed in connection with the application, shall be fined not more than $2,500.

Form SR-Full   Rev: 11/2006   Print: 11/2006—60,000   Printed on recycled paper   U.S. Government Printing Office: 2007-330-945/60,138

Page 4 of 4

BIBLIOGRAPHY

Bibliography and Recommended Reading

This Business of Music: Ninth Edition
By M. William Krasilovsky
Publisher: Billboard Books; 9th, Book only edition (June 1, 2003)
ISBN: 0823077284

Financial Management for Musicians
By Cathy McCormack and Pam Gaines
Publisher: ArtistPro,
ISBN: 0872887138

Booking, Promoting and Marketing Your Music
A Complete Guide for Bands and Solo Artists
By Nyree Belleville
Publisher: ArtistPro
ISBN: 0872887391

Get It In Writing
The Musician's Guide to the Music Business
By Brian McPherson
Publisher: Hal Leonard
ISBN: 0793566991

Ruthless Self-Promotion In the Music Industry
By Jeffrey P. Fisher
Publisher: ArtistPro,
ISBN: 0872887146

Build and Manage Your Music Career
By Maurice Johnson
Publisher: ArtistPro
ISBN: 0872887251

Music Producers—2nd Edition
Conversations with Today's Top Hit Makers!
Edited By Barbara Schultz
Publisher: ArtistPro
ISBN: 0872887308

Sonic Alchemy
Visionary Music Producers and Their Maverick Recordings
By David N. Howard
Publisher: Hal Leonard
ISBN: 0634055607

Networking Strategies for the New Music Business
Developing Successful Relationships in Today's Music Industry
By Dan Kimpel
Publisher: ArtistPro
ISBN: 1592007538

Succeeding In Music
A Business Handbook for Performers, Songwriters, Agents,
Managers & Promoters
By John Stiernberg
Publisher: Backbeat Books
ISBN: 0879307021

Build and Manage Your Music Career
By Maurice Johnson
Publisher: ArtistPro
HL 00330464